Living
Reconciliation

Phil Groves and
Angharad Parry Jones

Adapted by Paula Nesbitt

Published in 2014 by Forward Movement
412 Sycamore Street
Cincinnati, Ohio 45202
www.forwardmovement.org

First published in Great Britain in 2014
Society for Promoting Christian Knowledge
36 Causton Street
London SW1P 4ST
www.spckpublishing.co.uk

Forward Movement
www.forwardmovement.org

Living Reconciliation

Phil Groves and
Angharad Parry Jones

Adapted by Paula Nesbitt

Forward Movement
Cincinnati, Ohio

Table of Contents

A task for all
What is reconciliation?
Conflict and the church
Inhabiting reconciliation
Your story?
Following Peter

The first followers
Alice Mogwe

Clarity vs. reality
A journey into truth
Continuing Indaba journeys

Community in the followers of Jesus
Culture shock
Jesus crossing cultures
Jesus and the Samaritan woman
Crossing cultures
Forming journeying communities
Beyond respect

Jesus, Lord, King, and Messiah
Jesus meets the power question
Power and leadership
Redefining power
Foot-washing
Uncomfortable challenge
Including children
Including all

African or Lambeth *lectio*
New way of being

Foreword

Reconciliation is the heart of the gospel

Reconciliation is God's mission to the world in Christ; therefore it is our mission. It is one of the three priorities for my tenure as Archbishop of Canterbury, alongside the renewal of prayer and religious life, and evangelism. Reconciliation is at the heart of our calling to serve God in prayer and in witness. When we call on God out of the division and conflict of our world, God (as Karl Barth reminds us) "calls us to his side as heralds of reconciliation."[1] This book shows us how we may live at God's side in that exacting work, as reconciled reconcilers—in an era when it has possibly never been harder or more needful.

I believe that living reconciliation can transform our world. Indeed, I dream that it may become the hallmark of Anglicans. Given the cultural diversity of the 165 countries in which the Anglican Communion across 38 provinces exists—I believe that Anglican Christians bear remarkable testimony to the unifying power of the Holy Spirit of God in his Church. It is through our own reconciliation that the Holy Spirit equips us for the ministry of reconciliation and healing to others. Reconciliation is good news in a world of fear and alienation.

During my first eighteen months as archbishop, I have set out to visit the primates of each of the provinces in the Communion. Getting to know one another is surely a pre-requisite if we are to address the challenges of disagreement. Certainly it has proved a tangible way to express the mutuality of my relationship with those who lead and care for their churches within this family of God. The warmth of their welcome and hospitality has left a strong impression, and even more so, their faith and courageous witness—and ministry of reconciliation—among some of the poorest and most brutalized people on earth.

The experience with my fellow primates, their families and colleagues, has reawakened in me a sense of the privilege, responsibility, and opportunity we share as fellow-Anglicans. With all Christians everywhere, we are bound together by baptism and eucharist. Among Anglicans, the bonds of affection have been reinforced through our common and sometimes costly history, through (and sometimes despite) which a precious legacy of common worship, theology, and ministry have been forged.

In practical terms, this common legacy is spelled out in the five marks of mission, based on the conviction that the mission of the Church is the mission of Christ. First, we proclaim the

Good News of the Kingdom. Secondly, we teach, baptize, and nurture new believers. Thirdly, we respond to human need by loving service. In difficult places, fourthly, we continue to seek to transform unjust structures of society, to challenge violence of every kind, and to pursue peace and reconciliation. And in all of this, fifthly and finally, we are mindful of our responsibility to strive to safeguard the integrity of creation and sustain and renew the life of the earth.

We agree on these marks. Yet in so many other things, we disagree. Given our transparent and open structures, we often do so loudly. But we do so as part of a family, which however much it falls out, remains linked. We have to deal with the reality that no matter how strained the relationships may become at times, we belong to each other.

This makes all of our decision-making processes very complicated. As Anglicans we are both catholic and reformed: committed to a shared life together (our catholicity), yet retaining local autonomy (having neither pope nor curia). Thus we are deeply affected by one another, even though our diverse provinces remain technically independent and autonomous. When differences arise, therefore, there is no simple solution.

It is only as we listen deeply to one another, and learn about each other's context, that we can address effectively those things which most threaten to divide us. Inevitably there will be mistakes, misunderstanding, and miscommunication, despite best intentions. Where we disagree we need to ask ourselves: what is there of the gospel, of Jesus, in the view and life of those I disagree with?

Whether it is on matters of human sexuality or other things, what we each decide has impact on others around the world. I am not arguing that we should resist making decisions until the entire Anglican Communion (let alone the universal church) is in total and unanimous agreement. That would be a legalistic and regulatory response to a problem which is relational and missional.

Rather, I am eager to encourage each of us to take full account of the way in which decisions in one province echo around the world. We do not have a volume button that can limit or determine how our voices are heard beyond our own country or region. The impact of their echoes is something to which we must listen in the process of our decision-making, if we are not to narrow our horizons and reject the breadth of our global family. That process requires extensive conversation and prolonged engagement—an honest reinforcement of the bonds of relationship—amidst the confusing and costly work of common discernment.

Where does this leave us? It leaves us as pilgrims struggling through tough terrain, eager for clear direction from God while refusing to abandon others along the way. In other words, it leaves us facing reality, which defies an early or neat resolution because it is neither simple nor tidy; a reality for which we need help.

I welcome the publication of this book, a resource for that tough reality. Phil Groves and Angharad Parry Jones have brought to us the best learning from the work of Continuing Indaba. We can learn much from this experience around the Communion, not least for the Church of England as we enter a process of shared conversations on human sexuality.

Indaba is a Zulu term describing a traditional process for achieving mutual understanding in the midst of differences and disagreements. It has quickly become an invaluable gift for the global Communion. I was involved in the design of the project along with Anglicans from Southern Africa and elsewhere, drawing upon my experience from my time at Coventry Cathedral. I endorse it not because it has always got everything right—no process could do that—but because it has dared to invite us into a space where differences and disagreement are acknowledged in the diversity and unity of the family of God.

How we live with our deepest differences is probably the fundamental challenge of our time—for the world as well as the church. If, as the body of Christ, we can work out a way of disagreeing without dividing, then we will have much to offer the world. The gospel will gain credibility. As Christians, our belonging together cannot be purely a matter of institutional allegiance: it must be found in our mutual commitment to one another in Christ. Conversation together is not a diversion or delaying tactic, nor is it an outcome. It is a path to understanding, a way of walking together in faith, today. Ensuring that we relate together in a way that enables divergent voices to be heard and all of us to look to God is the biblical way to function.

A process of this nature comes with a cost. Entering conversations on areas of deep disagreement is not safe, for anyone, there is risk and vulnerability. A safe space is one where this cost is recognized and the space is entered and used respectfully. Diversity and difference cannot be wished away, even when their breadth makes us uncomfortable and at times unsafe.

People do change through dialogue: not necessarily in what they think but in how they act. Through the relationships established, they come to handle their views relative to others. At its best, dialogue changes how we talk with and about one another. Healthy relationships in which there is even a possibility of persuasion begin from such a place: by being emotionally correct. We may still not agree but we are listening to each other, not because of what we say but how we have said it. It is all too easy to be politically right but emotionally wrong; indeed, theologically right but relationally dysfunctional.

All this goes someway to articulate what we may mean when we speak of good disagreement. Good disagreement is informed disagreement. It is engaging in conversation with discretion and respect, to listen to and interpret the other in the light of their best intentions. It requires self-restraint in our public exchanges where other agendas may be at work. It is how we earn the right to have dialogue on the substance of our disagreement.

Through all our differences we belong to one another: not through our choice, but God's. Those who follow Christ are relatives—we are related through our Shepherd. You may choose your friends, but you are stuck with your relatives.

So we do not have the option, if we love one another in the way that Jesus instructs us, simply to ditch those with whom we disagree. You do not chuck out members of the family: you love them and seek their well-being, even when you argue. Good and loving disagreement is a potential gift to a world of bitter and divisive conflict. What can be more radical than to disagree well, not by abandoning principle and truth, but affirming it with respect? Acting on it and yet continuing to love those who have a different view?

Within the Anglican Communion we witness to our faith in many diverse cultures. The struggle, the achievement, of holding together in good disagreement sets a pattern in which truth is not a weapon with which to strike others, but a light freely offered for a path of joy and flourishing.

A global church, in which all Christians irrevocably belong to each other through the action of God and who seek to discern truth across the diversity of cultures represented, is a church with fuzzy edges. It is such a church which holds for the world the treasure of reconciliation, and offers it as a gift freely given out of its own experience of struggling with the reality of the cross. In the end, we know ourselves to be reconciled only through the sovereign love of God in Jesus Christ.

+Justin Cantuar, Trinity 2014

Acknowledgments

The writing of this book has been a journey. It was inspired by many journeys of reconciliation around the Anglican Communion, including the Continuing Indaba program. There are many people around the world to whom we are hugely grateful for setting us on the path to writing this book, for walking with us as our journey took shape, and for encouraging us along the way.

Those who set us on the path—the Compass Rose Society, for the generous support to get the idea off the ground; to SPCK, for their enthusiastic partnership; and to the Standing Committee of the Anglican Communion, for their ongoing support and encouragement.

Those who walked with us—all those involved in the Continuing Indaba journey, who wrote theological papers, traveled far and wide, offered hospitality, facilitated, evaluated, and more; those who shared their stories with us and allowed us to share their stories with you.

The small group from St. Mark's, Leamington Spa, who tried out the book chapter by chapter, asking the questions that guided our steps.

Our colleagues, friends, family, and our faith communities who encouraged us on our way. It's hard to single people out, but we'd like to thank the following by name: Joe Barlow, Natasha Barlow, David Chillingworth, Rani Clare, Cecelia Clegg, Cath Hollywell, Marcella King, Sarah Klein, Janet Marshall, Susan Mileham, Paul Mileham, Alice Mogwe, Joanna Moriaty, David Moxon, Mkunga Mtingele, Faith Natukunda, Philip Natukunda, Paula Nesbitt, John Mark Oduor, Hannah Reese, Jo Sadgrove, Rob Sommer, Deb Tammearu, Winnie Vargheese, Meg Warner, and Flora Winfield.

> O give thanks to the Lord, for he is good;
>   for his steadfast love endures forever.
> (1 Chronicles 16:34)

About the authors

Phil Groves and Angharad Parry Jones have worked together for the past five years at the Anglican Communion Office. Their work has been to organize and guide Continuing Indaba and to promote it within the Anglican Communion.

Phil Groves is a canon in Mpwapwa Diocese in Tanzania, where he served for six years, teaching and learning with the community at St. Philip's Theological College. He loves discovering cultures. His doctorate of philosophy was on partnership and explored the relationship between Paul and the community at Philippi. His dyslexia has been an advantage in gaining a deeper understanding of people and has enabled him to develop skills in problem-solving. In the Anglican Communion he served first as the facilitator for the Listening Process and then coordinated with others the design of Continuing Indaba.

Angharad Parry Jones hails from North Wales. Although she left at age twenty, she has remained very conscious of her Welshness. This doesn't just entail being a rugby fanatic and having a passion for the color red. It shapes her attitudes toward community, inclusion, and being on the side of the underdog. Prior to her work at the Anglican Communion Office, she was involved in mission with YWAM in her teens, has lived in an intentional community, and worked in Europe with the World Student Christian Federation on issues ranging from politics to gender in an ecumenical context.

* * *

Paula Nesbitt adapted the original text of *Living Reconciliation* for a North American audience. She is a priest in the Diocese of California and a scholar at the Graduate Theological Union. While serving as a research evaluator with Continuing Indaba, she also taught at the University of California, Berkeley. She has done field research at three Lambeth conferences.

Introduction

This book was inspired by Archbishop Justin Welby's sermon at the 2013 Faith in Conflict conference in Coventry, England, in which he urged all Christians to become reconciled reconcilers. It draws heavily on the stories, theology, and process from the Anglican Communion's Continuing Indaba program as well as other experiences. You can read more about both of these below or take a look at www.continuingindaba.com. This is not a book about the Continuing Indaba program itself. It does not describe what happened in detail, but it is a product of the learning and theology gained through that program.

Continuing Indaba and the Anglican Communion

American Bishop Stephen Bayne, who was the first executive officer of the Anglican Communion, from 1960 to 1964, found it impossible to define Anglicanism beyond a commitment to the Bible, the historic creeds, the sacraments of baptism and Holy Communion, and the leadership of bishops in succession to the apostles. Almost all churches agree on the first three and most agree on the fourth. This meant that he could find nothing unique to Anglicanism in any of these markers. Anglicanism was nothing more than an imperfect expression of the universal church.

The 1963 Anglican Congress defined relationships between the churches of the Anglican Communion as one of Mutual Responsibility and Interdependence (MRI) and from that Bayne argued that what actually defines Anglicans is that we meet as Anglicans. We form relationships across all kinds of divides—geography, culture, economics, language, and world-view—to be recognizably one Communion. It is reconciliation that enables us to be a communion of people who recognize Christ in one another while disagreeing on issues that have divided many churches.

Anglicans value different integrities and see that the whole is greater through the diversity we embrace. Anglicans meet in worship with one another while disagreeing on the theology of salvation, the sacraments, the use of vestments, and our theologies of ordination. Charismatic evangelical Anglicans in Kenya and liberal catholic Anglicans in Southern Africa ordain women as priests and can have women bishops. Conservative evangelicals in Nigeria and Anglo-Catholic Anglicans in Papua New Guinea do not ordain women. Each one makes its decision from a completely different theological starting point, but again and again they meet to worship the one Christ together as partners in the gospel. Reconciliation is at the heart of Anglicanism.

Over the past forty years the cherished diversity of the Anglican Communion has been tested to the limit. At first, many feared that the Communion would split over the decision of provinces such as Hong Kong, Canada, The Episcopal Church in the United States,[1] Uganda, and Kenya to ordain women to the priesthood.[2] Then, at the 1988 Lambeth Conference, Archbishop Robert Runcie wrestled with the fear that the impending consecration of women as bishops would create still deeper divisions.[3] In response, a doctrinal commission was appointed and given the task of discovering the best way Anglicans could hold together under such strains.[4]

The 1998 Lambeth Conference demonstrated the strength of feelings on human sexuality in the Communion. Many people believed the Communion would fracture with the consecration of an openly gay man in a partnership and the move by some dioceses and provinces to endorse the use of liturgies blessing gay partnerships. In 2005 the Anglican Communion published the Windsor Report with specific proposals aimed at maintaining a visible unity in the midst of conflict.

In the run-up to the 2008 Lambeth Conference, a number of models were suggested to enable the invited bishops to foster mutual responsibility and interdependence. At the suggestion of Archbishop Thabo Makgoba—a member of the Lambeth design team—the concept of Indaba was embraced as an alternative to the polemical parliamentary style of debating commonly used at Lambeth Conferences despite no precedent for it in scripture. Indaba was defined by him as "a gathering for purposeful discussion."[5]

The 2008 Lambeth Conference also received an interim report from the Windsor Continuation Group, which presented its final recommendations to the 2009 Primates' Meeting in Alexandria. One of the recommendations was:

> We need to move from intransigence and the conviction that "our" interpretation is the right one to a shared waiting upon God. There is something profoundly important about the Anglican Way here – a readiness to acknowledge that Christian disciples discern God's truth by learning to wait upon one another and that it takes the whole Church to know the whole truth.[6]

In response to the request of the Primates, the 2009 Anglican Consultative Council (ACC) voted to establish the Continuing Indaba project. This project aimed to develop a process that would:

- intensify relationships across the Communion

- energize local and global mission

- enable genuine conversation across difference.

The project began by inviting a number of theologians, pastors, and church leaders from across the theological spectrum to consultations in their own region. In each "hub" they worked together to develop theological resources to inform the process of seeking a common mind. By reflecting on scripture and the traditions of the church in the context of diverse cultures, with an emphasis on non-western cultures, Continuing Indaba collected insights from around the Anglican Communion.

These hubs were followed by four pilot conversations. Each one involved three dioceses chosen by the project directors in consultation with two facilitators and a team of three evaluators. Some dioceses came together for the first time. Others came as existing partnerships. Each diocesan team consisted of eight members who participated in encounters of at least a week, hosted by each diocese in turn. These were followed by a three-day facilitated conversation. The conversations were evaluated by a team of three social scientists and the results published.

The evaluation of the pilot conversations pointed to the effectiveness and potential of Continuing Indaba. The pilot project found that the Indaba method and experience are worthwhile in strengthening understanding and supporting mutual mission, and in building bonds of affection across the Anglican Communion. The need is now great for developing the kinds of resources that can reinforce the experience and help those who have participated to share and teach others.

Since the close of the conversations, the Continuing Indaba team has been promoting the use of the methods through contacts and through a website. This has led to dioceses and provinces examining how they live with conflict and value diversity. A number of provinces, dioceses, parishes, and groups with a common purpose have applied the Indaba process and resources in their own contexts, and ongoing learning continues to redefine the models.

Continuing Indaba offers a vision for the Anglican Communion to flourish in our common life. It is relationship-centered, beginning with people discovering common faith in different contexts. Relationships in Christ create safe space for difficult conversations on matters of significance, and promote constructive change in accord with a deepening journey of faith. The aim of participation in Continuing Indaba is for individuals and churches to be transformed in the image of Christ as described in 2 Corinthians 3:18:

> And all of us, with unveiled faces, seeing the glory of the Lord as though reflected in a mirror, are being transformed into the same image from one degree of glory to another; for this comes from the Lord, the Spirit.

Living Reconciliation Online

Additional material including videos, study guides, and further reading to accompany this book can be found at http://www.living-reconciliation.org.

Chapter 1

Living Reconciliation

In 2003 the Black Eyed Peas were a struggling Los Angeles-based hip-hop act seeking a hit. They had a core following and wanted to get into the mainstream. They had been working on a song for over a year and had a melody and a theme, but they wanted a hook and they wanted a superstar to front it. Most successful pop songs are about young love, but some mega hits rise above the ordinary to tap into deep social themes. The song the Black Eyed Peas were working on was a reflection on violence and injustice in America and around the world. They gave the song to international superstar Justin Timberlake and he loved it. He added a chorus and sang the key question—in a world of pain, "Where is the love?"

The Peas had their song, and they had their superstar-guarantee of success, but Timberlake was about to release an album and his record company refused permission for his name to be on a record that was so risky. It must have been a real slap in the face to the Peas. He was a co-writer, but not credited; he sang the chorus, and his face was not on the record cover. Remarkably, the record still sold. It was the Pea's first true hit, and it sold because it spoke into the hearts of those who heard it, not because of an endorsement. Most interestingly of all, it asked the question: are you willing "to practice what you preach?"

The story of the song, as much as the lyrics, is a great place to begin this book. We all have times when we look out to the world around us and ask the question "Where is the love?" We are tempted to place our hope in a global superstar, but we need to have confidence in ourselves. We need to join our voices with those superstars and see that the power for change is in the millions of people around the world who respond to the message. The question the song asks is the question asked by this book: Are you willing to be love in the world?

A common reaction to the violence and pain in all our societies is to think "this isn't my problem," and to assume that the way we live cannot make an impact on the world. Instead we long for mighty heroes of peace to swoop in and solve the conflicts that scar our world and bring about peace by the force of their personalities and the power of their words. The truth is that the world is changed by ordinary people living in a new way. Healthy, vibrant communities are created by the people who live in them. They are maintained by people constantly paying attention to the needs of one another. It is hard work. It demands commitment and requires perseverance.

There are heroes of peace and reconciliation, people like Nelson Mandela, Mahatma Gandhi, and Aung San Suu Kyi.

These people are global superstars, the people all politicians, rock stars, and sports people want to be associated with. We honor them and rejoice when they win the Nobel Peace Prize. We want their long walks to freedom, their years of incarceration, and their suffering to redeem our lives. Our participation in their struggle may only be to feel the emotion surging through us as we watch documentaries about them or attend rock concerts in their honor.

These heroes of peace know that the struggle they have been on is only of value if all participate. When the committee awarded the 2004 prize to Kenyan environmental and political activist Wangari Maathai, they said they did so because she represented "an example and a source of inspiration for everyone in Africa fighting for sustainable development, democracy, and peace."[1] The greatest of the Nobel Peace laureates stand for movements of ordinary people; they may be the figureheads, but the work is shared and they strive to inspire generations of people.

As Desmond Tutu said in his 1984 Nobel lecture:

> God calls us to be fellow workers with him, so that we can extend his kingdom of shalom, of justice, of goodness, of compassion, of caring, of sharing, of laughter, joy, and reconciliation, so that the kingdoms of this world will become the kingdom of our God and of his Christ, and he shall reign forever and ever. *Amen.*[2]

Peace prize winners are faced with a dilemma. We hold them up as heroes of peace, and we want to watch as they bring it about; they know from painful experience that peace is only achieved by all being involved. We want them to fix the world and end conflict; they know that they can do nothing without all of us playing our part.

This is not a new problem. It was precisely the problem that faced Jesus at the beginning of his ministry. Following his baptism, Jesus went alone to the desert where he was confronted with three temptations. In each of the three, Jesus is challenged by Satan to fix something or to take overall control. The first temptation offers Jesus the opportunity to make bread out of stone, thereby fixing the problem of hunger. The second temptation challenges Jesus to display his power by throwing himself off a building and come away unharmed, thereby demonstrating his miraculous power and superhuman abilities. This would elevate him to a place where he could exert dominating power over people. The third temptation is much more blatant in that he is offered the chance to rule. Who could argue with that? The all-loving Jesus ruling over all.

This interpretation was brought to life in the "Parable of the Grand Inquisitor," which is an essential part of Fyodor Dostoevsky's novel *The Brothers Karamazov*. In the novel the rationalist Ivan Karamazov challenges his religious brother

Aloysha though the recounting of a tale. It is set in Seville in the time of the Spanish Inquisition and in it Christ has returned and has been imprisoned. The Grand Inquisitor himself confronts Jesus and berates him for offering freedom when people want food, certainty, and to be told what to do. Jesus rejects the charge and again refuses the offer and kisses the Inquisitor, recalling the kiss between Judas and Jesus.

When Jesus leaves the desert, he has chosen to reject the possibilities of dominating power. He rejects the power to weigh in and impose change—to fix things. Instead, the first thing Jesus does is to find people who will walk with him. Throughout his ministry, and in particular during the last few weeks of his life, Jesus encountered the expectation of those around him that as Messiah he would fix things, call upon an army of angels, and just make everything all right. Jesus rejected that temptation. In his life, teachings, death, and resurrection, he invites his followers into a new way of being.

Throughout this book we are going to consider Living Reconciliation as a task entrusted to each and every one of us—not just to special people. It is not only for those interested in justice and peace; it is integral to the Christian message. Paul is emphatic about this:

> So if anyone is in Christ, there is a new creation: everything old has passed away; see, everything has become new! All this is from God, who reconciled us to himself

through Christ, and has given us the ministry of reconciliation; that is, in Christ God was reconciling the world to himself, not counting their trespasses against them, and entrusting the message of reconciliation to us. (2 Corinthians 5:17–19)

We invite you to explore with us what Living Reconciliation as a follower of Jesus Christ means for all of us. This is not a book about reconciliation; it is aimed at helping us to live a life of reconciliation.

We know that this is challenging. While we celebrate the lives of those who brought peace and reconciled nations, we also know that at times we all avoid conflict, distrust diversity, and seek out those who agree with us. We ask you to take up the challenge to be constantly asking and responding to the question "Where is the love?" as you Live Reconciliation.

What is reconciliation?

Reconciliation is difficult to define, but it can be described by the stories of people who live it. Stories help us to understand the meaning in a deeper way and to think about it. Throughout this book, you will be asked to enter into stories that will help you Live Reconciliation. So, we begin with a story.

Imagine a school playground fight. When the playground erupts to the shouts of "Fight! Fight!" the teachers' primary goal is to break up the spat, disperse the crowd, and find out who started it. They assert their authority to separate the children and then seek to gain a common account of the dispute. Power is deferred to the adult in authority and the immediate problem is solved. However, if the teacher does not address the reason for the fight, lingering tensions and divisions remain. The immediate conflict might be resolved by punishment, but it is not the end in itself. Reconciliation occurs when the children apologize and forgive each other and all return to playing with one another. Reconciliation here is marked by the children laughing together, not by the cold administration of justice. The conflict becomes transformed when the teacher acts as a facilitator of reconciliation rather than an arbiter of justice.

The pattern of fight, forced separation, judgment, and reconciliation is played out in every community around the world. It also highlights the issues at the heart of conflict resolution and transformation.

In November 1940, the beautiful medieval sandstone cathedral in the city of Coventry burned to the ground as the bombs from German war planes ignited the roof's ancient wooden frame. Across the United Kingdom the blitz evoked emotions of anger and revenge that expressed itself toward the end of the war in the destruction of the beautiful German city of Dresden. In stark contrast to the mood of the era, Coventry Cathedral's Provost Dick Howard made a commitment not to revenge, but to forgive. The words "Father Forgive" were inscribed on the wall of the ruined chancel as a confession of the common human need for God's mercy. He resisted all attempts to insert the word "them" at the end of the statement.

The words were matched by simple acts of deep symbolism. Two charred beams had fallen in the shape of a cross, and these were placed behind an altar of rubble. Three large medieval nails were formed into a cross. Such symbols define reconciliation as clearly as any words. The death of the cathedral was linked to a sign of hope, the empty cross—the symbol not only of the death of Christ but also his resurrection. The cross was an extreme instrument of torture that in its association with Christ became a sign of blessing. The challenge was, and is, how can a destroyed building be part of that same story?

The Cross of Nails is central to the reconciliation ministry associated with Coventry Cathedral. Replicas of the nails are placed in a piece of actual stone from the bombed cathedral and sent to churches and chapels around the world as a focal point for communities committed to Living Reconciliation. Those who display the cross share a common commitment to work and pray for peace, justice, and reconciliation through:

- healing the wounds of history
- learning to live with difference and celebrate diversity
- building a culture of peace.

These Coventry commitments are not a definition of reconciliation: they are a mandate for action. Those who Live Reconciliation never stop learning more about it. Living Reconciliation is painful, risky, difficult work that makes all who participate vulnerable. Ever since 1940 the Community of Coventry Cathedral has been on a journey exploring the implications of the commitment to reconciliation. Since 1974 they have been joined by people throughout the world in the Community of the Cross of Nails. On every step of the way, they are reminded that reconciliation is the heart of the gospel. Reconciliation is not an aspect of Christian living for a few enthusiasts. It is the gospel.

Texts such as 2 Corinthians 5:17–19 and Colossians 1:19–20 are often quoted in support of the idea that reconciliation is at the heart of the gospel. However, reconciliation runs through the entire Bible. The story of the Bible is the story of reconciliation.

Reconciliation is more than ending conflict. For Paul, reconciliation is breaking down the barriers that separate us from God and from one another, and living in community once those barriers are removed. In his letter to the Philippians, Paul celebrates Jesus reconciling humanity to God, not by exploiting his divinity but through humility and death:

> [Jesus] emptied himself, taking the form of a
> slave, being born in human likeness.
> And being found in human form, he

> humbled himself and became obedient to
> the point of death—even death on a cross.
> (Philippians 2:7–8)

The barrier between God and humanity was then broken. In Romans 8, Paul describes Jesus' resurrection as a declaration of victory of the law of life over the law of sin and death (verse 2). It is this victory that gives Paul the courage to declare:

> For I am convinced that neither death, nor life,
> nor angels, nor rulers, nor things present, nor
> things to come, nor powers, nor height, nor
> depth, nor anything else in all creation, will
> be able to separate us from the love of God in
> Christ Jesus our Lord. (Romans 8:38–39)

This victory was confirmed when the Holy Spirit came with power, enlivening the people of God and breaking down the barriers that separated people from each other. On the day of Pentecost, everyone heard the good news in their own language. No longer was there one special people with one language who were set apart: God is God of the whole world, of Jew and Gentile, men and women, slave and free. The Holy Spirit did not destroy diversity but challenged the church to embrace it.

In the world in which we live, societies construct barriers that separate us from one another. We live behind walls of language, culture, economics, personality, age, and gender. The destruction of these barriers helps us to form friendships and to live as a community of diversity while retaining our distinct identities in the Body of Christ. This means that reconciliation does not end; it is a journey of exploration and learning that requires listening and speaking. It requires us to trust one another and God.

But we keep on erecting barriers. We sometimes do so for the best of motives. Just like the teacher separating children on a playground, barriers are erected to contain people and ensure that they do not fight one another. Peacekeeping can be the act of erecting barriers so that a vulnerable group feels safe. Mediation may be the way to negotiate across those barriers. Reconciliation happens when the barriers are removed and people can speak to one another face to face, encounter difference, and live with healthy conflict. It requires repentance and forgiveness on a lifelong journey in community.

Reconciliation is not an action; it is a way of being. It is a life into which we are called, not something we achieve and then move on. We celebrate this week by week in the eucharist. Eucharistic worship begins with confession and forgiveness, leads to reconciliation with one another in the peace, and focuses on the story of reconciliation remembered in words and experienced in bread and wine, body, and blood. The worship ends with the sending out into the world to live that peace.

Conflict and the church

Passionate conflicts are part of every dynamic, growing church. The letters to New Testament churches were almost all written in the context of conflict. The church in Corinth had split into factions; the churches in Galatia and in Ephesus were struggling with those who sought to impose Jewish laws on the whole body; and the Christians addressed by John the Apostle were saying they loved God while showing disdain for one another. Conflict in churches is nothing new.

Churches are full of people, and people argue. They quarrel over the most seemingly trivial things such as the placing of flowers following a funeral, the kind of music played in a service, or the state in which the kitchen was left by one group or another. We also quarrel about serious issues of theology and practice and other matters that mean something fundamental to us. We are passionate in our disagreement.

Conflict is healthy. It challenges complacency and confronts injustice. It was an essential element of the East African Revival, which became an important Protestant renewal movement. Ordinary Christians were encouraged to call one another to account, and clergy—including bishops—to faithfulness. In South Africa the move from racist institution to rainbow church required face-to-face conflict before reconciliation could occur. The church was a place where white, black, and colored could be together, but overcoming inbuilt prejudice was uncomfortable for all.

Conflict within and between churches can be very destructive. At its worst, it can lead to war, as has often been the case in Europe. It also can lead to the kind of murderous sectarianism that has scarred Northern Ireland. Unhealthy conflict is a frightening prospect, but it also can be a driving force for seeking an alternative way to be together.

The Anglican Communion has experienced both healthy conflict and that considered to be evil. Many like to use the calm reasonableness of sixteenth-century theologian Richard Hooker to define the Church of England. We sometimes forget that century was marked by years of vicious bloodletting, with Anglicans on different sides of the theological divides prepared not only to renounce but also to execute their opponents for believing the wrong doctrines. The present tensions between evangelical and catholic, liberal and conservative, are for many people a sign of health in this and other churches that have managed to hold together people who have views that divided other churches.

Over recent years, a number of issues have highlighted deep divisions within Anglicanism. News stories have focused on conflict within and between churches of the Anglican Communion over female priests and bishops, and the inclusion of lesbian/gay/bisexual/transgender (LGBT) people. The history of these conflicts is charted in numerous books and on Internet sites. No single account of the story is uncontested, and it is impossible to write such a history without accusations of bias.

What has surprised many people is that the Anglican Communion has not split apart. Like the church in Corinth there are many factions and groups, but few have been decisive and many relationships have remained in place across those divisions. This means that the Anglican Communion has a story to tell—a story of a rocky, uncertain journey that has been marked by times where people have come face to face with people they disagree with profoundly and discovered that they cannot merely abandon them. They have recognized Christ in one another and resolved to struggle with the difficult question of how to read the scriptures together and to share bread and wine with one another.

A turning point came at the 2008 Lambeth Conference. Every ten years the Archbishop of Canterbury has invited all bishops of the Communion to join him to consider a wide range of issues and concerns. In 2008 the conference abandoned its previous parliamentary style and adopted instead a relational process described by Archbishop Thabo Makgoba as "Indaba." The aim was to provide opportunities for the bishops to listen to one another and share ideas that would help them to be more effective leaders in mission when they returned to their own dioceses. He explained Indaba as "a gathering for purposeful discussion."[3]

Inhabiting reconciliation

In 2009 Archbishop Nzimbi of Kenya welcomed a number of Kenyan and Tanzanian theologians to a consultation in Limuru to take the next step after the 2008 Lambeth Conference and to continue the Indaba. The group consisted of lay and ordained women and men. They expected to be asked about human sexuality, but they were asked this question: How do you as African Anglicans understand processes of transforming conflict?

What happened was in itself a point of transformation. The conversation became tense and difficult as the Kenyans began to recognize that the real issue before them was not the worldwide Anglican divisions on human sexuality, but the scars emanating from ethnic violence that had erupted in their nation only twelve months earlier. In the room was a Kikuyu woman who had witnessed the violence perpetuated on her friends in Mombasa, a non-Kikuyu town. She had hidden away for two days, terrified that the door to her flat would be kicked in and she would be humiliated, raped, and killed, as had happened to many others. In the room too was a Luo woman who had been forced to flee a Kikuyu town, frightened of persecution by fellow Anglicans.

Reconciliation was not irrelevant; it was central to their future life together. This was the reality in the room, in the Anglican Church of Kenya, and in the nation. Those who were there stopped and prayed, and some cried. It was clear that people who had been living together for a year had not been able to speak to one another. They had been faculty and students in the same university—and had avoided the conflict. Suspicion could burn and anger smoulder under the surface. Trust was thin, even among people who shared the eucharist together. They began to see value in the processes of Indaba described by Archbishop Thabo Makgoba. When they replaced the word Indaba with the Swahili equivalent—*Baraza*—they took ownership of the process. They then began to design processes for themselves and for the Anglican Communion.

In November of the same year, they returned to the same room to offer and receive the work they had prepared individually and in groups. Over a twenty-four-hour period eighteen papers were presented, critiqued, and received. Some of these papers stand as significant signposts, shaping the future of the Anglican Communion through their contribution to the development of the emerging Continuing Indaba project. But more significantly, they addressed the immediate issues they were facing in their own contexts.

A paper by the Rev. John Mark Oduor brought the whole room alive as he set out the mandate for the making of a new drum to sound a new beat. He identified that in Kenya the loudest drum was calling people to war in church and state. The new drum needed to sound out a beat that "summons the community to a *Baraza*, under the tree of meeting; the Cross of Christ, for the healing, reconciliation, and unity of the community and the world."[4] Oduor wrote unashamedly as a Luo, as did others such as Dr. Emily Onyango. Their insights were matched by the thoughts of Kikuyu theologians such as the Rev. Dr. Sammy Githuku and the Ven. Dr. Ndung'u Ikenye. These paved the way for a Baraza of Kenyan bishops who, in facing one another across ethnic divides, were able to create a changed atmosphere in the run-up to the 2012 elections.

The event was transformative and gave direction for the future of the Continuing Indaba project in three distinct ways. First, it was understood that it is impossible to find a global solution to the conflicts in the Anglican Communion without, in the words of Bishop John Simalenga, "treating the roots of division in our own dioceses and parishes."[5] The local could not be ignored in the search for the global. Second, there are resources within the Bible for conflict transformation that had been previously ignored as the Communion relied on methods that were rooted in European culture. Stories from the Pentateuch, the Gospels, and the Letters were considered through the lens of African cultures and found to have rich insights into how we could Live Reconciliation. Third, bishops were not able to solve the problems alone. Lay and ordained people, some who were doctors of theology and others who were church workers, all had ideas to share and energy to give in Living Reconciliation.

Your story?

As we held other consultations across the Anglican Communion, these insights from Kenya were reinforced.

The local is the place to start. Living reconciliation begins with each of us in our own local contexts finding ways to face the conflicts in our own communities, and between our community and others. So we are inviting you, the reader, to participate in the journey of reconciliation—both locally and globally. There are two requirements. First, your journey must take place in relationship with others. Second, it must be lived out daily.

Two companions for your journey of Living Reconciliation are scriptures and stories. While stories occur in scripture, they also arise out of our own culture and experience. The collected perspectives of African, Asian, and Indigenous North American theologians are vital in opening up the scriptures in a new way, and this book aims to help you gain an understanding of their insights through stories. But the greatest stories are still those of the people who traveled with Jesus to the cross and who then traveled on with the Holy Spirit.

Most of the Bible is story, for a good reason. The great themes such as reconciliation are difficult to define, but they can be recognized in the lives of the people in the Bible and as lived by you. Stories bring these themes to life and give us much to think about in relation to our own lives.

The Bible forms the backbone and central focus of this book, as a guide on your journey of developing your own story of Living Reconciliation. Just as a guidebook to a great city means more once you are actually standing in front of a building it describes, this book will only come to life as you step out on the journey. It will be challenging but also rewarding. To help you throughout this book we are going to pick up the story of one particular companion of Jesus: Peter. We begin with an overview of his journey into Living Reconciliation.

Following Peter

Peter's journey with Jesus in life, death, and resurrection is full of moments of confidence and doubt, of getting it right and getting it wrong, each moment drawing himself and us deeper into Christ's story of reconciliation. By entering into Peter's journey, we can explore what it means for us to be drawn by Christ into this story of reconciliation.

As with his brother Andrew and their fishing partners James and John, Peter's journey with Jesus begins with watching. As they travel around with Jesus, they see miracles and hear him teaching; they are following Jesus and discovering more about this charismatic man who asked them to drop their nets and fish for people instead. Peter begins as a disciple (literally, one who follows) but things change when Jesus appoints him as one of the Twelve Apostles (literally, one who is sent out).[6] From this point, Peter and the other apostles are drawn into the mission and ministry of Jesus; they are watchers no longer, but workers with Jesus. It is in the account of Jesus walking on water [7] that we first encounter Peter's trademark enthusiasm and uncertainty. When Peter recognizes Jesus, in the midst of the storm and fear, he has every confidence in his friend and steps out of the boat. When he takes his eyes off Jesus and realizes what he's doing, then his doubts prevail and he begins to sink. This combination of enthusiastic faith and distracted doubt is characteristic of Peter in the gospels.

Perhaps the best-known example is the turning point in Jesus' ministry as he sets his face to Jerusalem. Peter proclaims that Jesus is the Messiah and then rebukes Jesus for talking about his own death (Mark 8:27–37). This is followed by another key Peter moment at the Transfiguration. As Jesus is transfigured into a dazzling white figure and is joined by Moses and Elijah, Peter's enthusiasm and uncertainty seem almost to frighten away the two prophets as he offers to enshrine the experience (Mark 9:2–13).

Key to Peter's journey with Jesus is the constant refrain, not of getting it right and then getting it wrong, but in thinking he has got it—he has arrived—only to realize that the journey with Jesus never ends. When we read of Jesus' radical action in washing his disciples' feet we see further into Peter's world (John 13:1–17). Peter is shocked at Jesus' behavior; as their teacher and master, it is Jesus' place to be served and be washed, not to serve and wash. In Peter's rebuke of Jesus there are echoes of the rebuke following his declaration of Jesus as the Christ—it is "the voice of sense" telling Jesus he's got things wrong. Jesus' rebuke of Peter is no less harsh here than it was then; it is in effect saying, "No, Peter, you're the one who's got it wrong—this is my way." Peter's enthusiasm returns, and he asks Jesus not only to wash his feet but the rest of him as well. He has a moment of realization that there is more about Jesus than he understands but has missed his role in Jesus' mission and ministry. As an apostle he has already been sent out by Jesus, has already been commissioned, but it is not until after Jesus' death and resurrection and the coming of the Holy Spirit at Pentecost that Peter is able to understand that role.

Peter's most famous action in the gospels is probably his denial of Jesus.[8] This too gives us a key insight into his character and his journey with Jesus in life, death, and resurrection: a journey full of moments of confidence and doubt, of getting it right and getting it wrong, each moment drawing himself and us deeper into Christ's story of reconciliation. When Jesus tells Peter that he will deny him, Peter's response is emphatic, declaring that he would die with Jesus before denying him. Yet, just as on the waters of the Sea of Galilee, when fear and the distractions of reality divert Peter from Jesus' promise and mission, he sinks and denies all relationship with Jesus. It is in the post-resurrection account of Jesus appearing to the fishing disciples back on the Sea of Galilee that we find the final part of this story. Peter, on seeing Jesus, in a characteristic fit of enthusiasm, leaps into the sea and swims to meet his friend. We can imagine that, as they are eating together, Peter begins to remember Jesus foretelling his betrayal and remembering his own words from the High Priest's courtyard, denying any knowledge of this man now sitting opposite him. In asking him over and over to "feed my sheep," Jesus is both forgiving Peter and reminding him of his role as an apostle—to be sent out.

It is not, however, until the Holy Spirit descends on the disciples at Pentecost that Peter finally has the courage to step into the role of an apostle, of one who is sent out (Acts 2:1–41). Since the death of Jesus, the apostles had become insular and isolated even though Jesus had appeared in their midst. They remained hidden and afraid behind locked doors. Their focus on electing Matthias as a replacement for Judas in response to Jesus' Ascension is indicative of the human need to keep things the same. There is an echo here of Peter's desire to build dwellings on the Mount of Transfiguration. However, when Peter is filled with the Holy Spirit, his calling to be an apostle is truly ignited. He addresses the crowd which has gathered to see the commotion, not as a follower defending a teaching but as one sent out by the teacher on a journey to share the good news.

Agents of reconciliation are often seen as betrayers of the communities they come from and heroes of the opposition. Peter found this out. It was Peter who first discovered that "God does not show favoritism and accepts women and men of every nation." It was Peter who argued this in front of the Council in Jerusalem headed by James the brother of Jesus. However, twenty years later he found himself susceptible to bullying. When he was in Antioch, living with both Gentile and Jewish Christians, a group came from James in Jerusalem and they intimidated him so that he refused to sit with Gentile Christians and convinced others to do the same. Paul opposed him publically and directly. Speaking to him face to face, Paul highlighted his hypocrisy and contrasted the following of Jesus in a faith relationship to the following of laws that end in death.

We learn from journeying with Peter that as Christians we are called into this journey of reconciliation—a journey that is marked not by its destination but by the landmarks encountered and relationships formed along the way. It is a journey full of risk and challenge, but it is one on which Christ calls us, challenges us, comforts, and commissions us. We are not called to be flawless, because like Peter we are going to get things wrong, but to be open to constantly learning, to be drawn further in by Jesus and to look beyond our immediate horizons. The first task is to hear the call and embark on the journey.

* * *

Prayer

> Loving God, who in Christ lived partnership
> between human and Divine to the full,
> call us, challenge us, and commission us
> in your work of reconciliation in the world.
> *Amen.*

Questions to think about

1. How does Peter's journey of trying, getting it right, and getting it wrong draw you deeper into Jesus' story?

2. How might you describe to others an incident that brings reconciliation for you in your life, your family, your nation, or your church?

3. Can you see from your experience those times when conflict has been valuable within your church or community?

Further thinking

For additional material on the topics discussed in this chapter—including videos, study guides, and further reading—please visit www.living-reconciliation.org.

Chapter 2

Journey into uncertainty

When the primates of the Anglican Communion met in Dublin in 2011 they made this commitment to one another:

> In our common life in Christ we are passionately committed to journeying together in honest conversation. In faith, hope, and love we seek to build our Communion and further the reign of God.[1]

In the first chapter we described Living Reconciliation as a journey, and in this chapter we will encourage you to set out on your journey. Living Reconciliation is not easy. It requires abandoning old securities and certainties and trusting in God. The journey into reconciliation is a journey into uncertainty.

This does not mean that there is uncertainty about the destination. The primates describe it as "furthering the reign of God." The motivation for the journey is the hope of resurrection, which is the sure foundation for all we do. Sometimes this can seem to be a long way off, but it is the

..omise that energizes those who work for peace in the face of the deepest despair.

We do not walk alone. We walk with God, following Christ in the power of the Spirit. We are also in the company of others who are Living Reconciliation, and we are inspired by the people we meet along the way. We are sustained by prayer, worship, and the study of the scriptures.

But we need to get going, and this is not easy. We have to leave the security of the familiar. Jesus called many people to follow him, but few were able to take up the challenge. One reason the first step was so difficult was because it meant placing trust in a person, not in a constructed system of beliefs and values. We are asking you to join in this same journey.

The first followers

When they accepted the call, the first followers of Jesus seem to have had almost no understanding of what they were doing or who they were following. Luke's Gospel tells us that Andrew had been a disciple of John the Baptist, and so he and his brother Peter may have had some idea of the life of a disciple. Even so, nothing could have prepared them for what their journey with Jesus might entail. It is all too tempting to imagine that Peter and Andrew, and James and John, were poor fishermen scraping an existence for themselves, but it's far more likely that the opposite was true. Fishing was big business around the Sea of Galilee. As partners in a fishing boat, these men employed laborers and were an essential part of the local economy. By putting down tools and walking away from this responsibility, Peter and Andrew, James and John took a giant leap into the journey of following Jesus. Whether he was rich or poor, Peter was committing himself to an uncertain future.

It is only deep into the journey that Peter suddenly articulates to Jesus and to himself the enormity of what he has done. In Mark 10, a rich man approaches Jesus supposedly seeking advice on how to gain eternal life. In reality he is seeking approval of his religious living. When Jesus calls him to give up his accumulated wealth, he turns away. Jesus then confounds the hopes of even his closest disciples by declaring the great difficulty of the rich entering the kingdom of God. It is Peter who then says, "Look, we have left everything and followed you." The implication is that Peter may have been expecting fame and fortune on the way, which is not what Jesus offers. It is almost an exclamation of despair.

When the first disciples began to follow Jesus, they did so without evidence or any guarantee of success. Others flocked for the miracles. But when Jesus disappointed them by offering words rather than bread, thousands turned away in scorn. Jesus asked the twelve disciples if they also wished to go away. Again it was Peter who said, "Lord, to whom can we go? You have the words of eternal life. We have come to believe and know that you are the Holy One of God."[2] It was only on the journey that Peter knew who he was following and why. When he set out, he'd had no idea.

Setting out on a journey of reconciliation is a step of faith. It requires trusting Jesus and leaving behind the certainties we know. It may not involve actual traveling, but it does involve reconsidering the ties that bind and embracing a new way. It involves getting to your feet and being inspired to act. During our time working with Continuing Indaba, we encountered and worked with some amazing people who did just that. Their lives are defined and shaped by living out Christ's call for reconciliation. One of them is Alice Mogwe, founder and director of DITSHWANELO, the Botswana Centre for Human Rights.

Alice Mogwe

When Alice signed up to study law at the University of Cape Town in the apartheid South Africa of the 1980s, she was offered an opportunity open to few other black Africans. The segregated education system in South Africa meant that students were generally denied their freedom to choose where and what to study. Educated in the United Kingdom as well as in her homeland of Botswana, Alice was among the elite. She also was living in a country that has known peace, prosperity, and independence since 1966. However, being black, suddenly the color of her skin meant something as she encountered the humiliating rules and regulations of life under apartheid. The experience challenged the way she saw the world. Up until then she had been optimistic about the power of the law to define a healthy community, but in South Africa she saw the law defending entrenched power and diminishing the lives of those who lived there.

Alice could have had an easy life and been among the comfortable middle class. But in 1993 she founded a human rights organization, and she has constantly championed the cause of the oppressed within her country. Although Alice is charming, a joy to be with, time and time again she challenges her own people.

The majority of people in Botswana are the Tswana, a Bantu group with links to numerous tribes across Africa. There are other communities of people in Botswana too. There remains a whisper of the ancient past, a group that has lived by hunting game and gathering berries as all humans did before they embraced agriculture. Squeezed onto land not suitable for farming, they represent only 4 percent of the population. They could have been safely ignored. But for all kinds of reasons, including the desire to have areas protected so rich people could see animals in the wild, it was decided for them that they were to be moved into settlements and taught to farm.

Throughout the 1990s, the "Bushmen," as they accept being called, were moved off the land. In the case of the Central Kalahari Game Reserve (CKGR), when they refused to leave, the government relocated essential services, which included the provision of water and food rations, to settlements where it wanted the people to live.

Embarking on an epic journey, an elder named Amogelang made his way to Alice to tell her that his people were thirsty. He and his family had no water and were surviving by eating moisture-laden plants. She listened to his story, and her reaction formed a significant part of a future legal strategy. Amogelang became a key witness in the CKGR case that ended in a high court decision in 2006. The government could remove the water and dehydrate the people in order to move them to land set aside for them.

The case was taken up by several western-based human rights organizations, but Alice observed that the process was disabling to the people. It led to the "Bushmen" being sidelined by both sides. For a start, the "Bushmen" were labeled by names they did not accept for themselves. Officially they were known as the "Basarwa," which is a Tswana word meaning "those who don't have cattle," and in that cultural context it is intended to make them seem both ridiculous and poor. In court the human rights lawyers fought for them, but there was no translation into their language.

When they spoke of "their land," the government lawyers asked them to prove ownership and demanded to see the paperwork. The elder replied that God had not given him papers. His grandfather and his grandfather's grandfather did not have papers. For him it was just the land they lived on, and the idea that anyone owned land was ridiculous. The rules by which their fate was settled were not rules they understood or endorsed.

Alice wanted a different approach than the western-style adversarial legalism. She wanted to use African methods and to engage in consensual conversations. She used her contacts and her influence to engage the people holding power in direct conversation with a thirsty man. Alice persuaded a government minister to sit in the same room as the elder, with her present to facilitate the conversation. The minister was no longer faced with an issue, but with a human being. Here was Amogelang who was seeking water to live. He was not seeking to be dependent or to have special provision. He was just asking for the water that had been provided for them by the government for several years.

The government changed its position and was ready to issue permits for the transport of the water so that the people could take it to their traditional homes. However, this was not good enough for Alice. She knew from her time in apartheid South Africa that permission is not a right and permits can be removed. Government ministers change, and foreign campaigners find new causes. New multinational corporations find clever lawyers to enforce their will on the community.

Around the world, a campaign began for water to become a human right. This was not the right to free water; it was the right to have access to water—even if it had to be paid for. Lined against it were multinational corporations ready to locate water-thirsty factories in semi-arid regions. It held serious implications for their profits, not only in Africa but also in places such as California. The United States government opposed granting access to water as a human right, and the battle was long and hard. It also took dedication and perseverance to convince the United Nations that access to water is a human right. It wasn't until the 2010 UN General Assembly that access to water was recognized, and today it is acknowledged as a human right in 122 countries.

For some Alice is a hero, and she has won several international awards. For some of her friends in Botswana, she is a maverick. Unlike many prosperous Batswana, she does not work for her own interests. She has brought to light injustice most people would not want to think about. Taking up the challenge to Live Reconciliation can be a lonely task; one where you can be in conflict with your own people. For Alice it involved identifying with those who were not her own people and having the courage to step back from advocating on their behalf in order to empower them to speak for themselves in their own way.

This is the journey Jesus experienced. He spoke with many who were not his people, separated by gender and ethnic barriers. And he was abused and rejected by his own people. This is the journey on which he called his companions to follow him, and the journey he calls us all to participate in—a journey of justice and reconciliation.

Alice was transformed by her experience into a person who saw beyond the certainties of her own community. As a young woman training to be a lawyer, she believed in the power of the law. But law can be easily confused with truth, and the truth is not always clear. Western legal and parliamentary processes are aimed at gaining clarity. The paper held by the government lawyers in Botswana clearly demonstrated who owned the land and who held the right to determine who lived there. The truth was not so clear. The "Bushmen" had been living on the land for centuries, and for them it was not even clear that land could be "owned." They had no paper, but their memories of the stories of their great grandparents told them they had been there before the papers in the hands of the lawyers had existed. The law courts of Botswana could offer a clear articulation of the law, but the truth was far more complex.

Living Reconciliation requires a crossing of cultural world-views that challenges some of our basic ways of thinking. Things we believe to be true may not be as certain as we once thought. It also requires us to put aside clarity in the interest of truth, even when such clarity has guided our lives.

This is the reason that Jesus taught in parables. One day a teacher of the law pressed Jesus for clarity on how to inherit eternal life. He wanted clear instructions, and he wanted to enter into a debate on the details of the rules and regulations. Jesus instead turned the question back on him, asking what was written in the law. When Jesus agreed with his answer that it was to love God completely and to love your neighbor as yourself, the lawyer was embarrassed by the simplicity. He quickly asked for clarification, asking for the definition of a neighbor. Frustrating to anyone who seeks clarity, Jesus responded with the story of the Good Samaritan.[3] The story is often used to highlight the hypocrisy of the religious. But the teacher of the law would know that to retain ritual purity, the priest and Levite would pass by on the other side of the road, and not help the badly injured man. The shock of the story is not that they behaved in the way they did; the shock is that following the law was not considered the good choice. In the story, the unclean Samaritan becomes the hero by helping the man. In the telling of the story, Jesus breaks down barriers of religious law that defined the identity of his listeners.

At the conclusion of the parable, Jesus has not given an answer to the teacher of the law. Instead he responds with another question: "Which of these three, do you think, proved to be a neighbor to the man who fell among the robbers?" When the man who placed his hope on obeying clear law replies with the words "The one who showed him mercy," he is told to do the same. He is told to Live Reconciliation and to love others across barriers of ethnicity and religion. He is to abandon clarity in favor of a journey into mercy.

If the journey of reconciliation is not defined by clarity, how can it be a journey that leads us into truth? One of the questions often asked by committed Christians as they embark on reconciliation is, "Will I be required to change my mind?" There is a fear that in Living Reconciliation truth will be put to one side in the interest of compromise. A middle way can be one that abandons all principle. In his sermon at the 2013 Faith in Conflict conference in Coventry, Archbishop Justin Welby reflected:

> I find myself often doubting myself deeply: have I become totally woolly, taken in by the niceness of bad people or bad theology, trapped in an endless quest for illusory peace rather than tough answers? That is a question that all involved in reconciliation should be asked, and held accountable to, but it is also part of the process.[4]

People fear that they will be forced to accept as legitimate the view of someone they not only disagree with, but whose value system is threatening to their essential beliefs. If they are told that they are hateful for not accepting women as priests, or faithless for accepting gay marriage, they may fear being forced into abandoning either friends or principles.

In contrast, Jesus did not tell the teacher of the law to become a Samaritan. He was not asked to embrace the value systems and beliefs of the Samaritan people; he was asked to live a life of love. We may think of Samaritans as wonderful, caring people. In reality, Samaritans are a community of people clearly defined by their religious beliefs that emerged from their reading of the Hebrew scriptures. For a Jew, Samaritans were heretics. In commending the action of one Samaritan, Jesus is not demanding that one set of clear rules should be replaced with another; he is questioning the correlation between rigid structures and the way of love.

Christians hold passionately to those doctrines and practices that define our faith. We share a faith in one God, Father, Son, and Holy Spirit, but we disagree on all kinds of things, large and small. We disagree on the nature and number of the sacraments. We disagree on the role of women and men in leadership and as priests or ministers. Not all Christians agree on the dates for Easter and Christmas. All of these things have split churches. Christians base their faith on the Bible but disagree on the meaning of the words and the methods of interpretation. Biblical scholars often find fault with one another on most matters of substance. Commentaries are written to help us understand the text, but in recent years they have grown longer and longer as more and different interpretations are proposed, refuted, and modified.

Living Reconciliation does not mean putting aside our beliefs. It means something far more threatening; it means recognizing that the person you believe to be completely wrong on some issue of significance is on a journey with Christ and with you.

It means trusting God together and not seeking to overwhelm or change the other with the force of your argument. It does mean being open to change, but to a change of heart and a desire to understand more fully your own walk with Christ.

A true process of reconciliation will allow all participating to "speak the truth in love" and encourage all to "grow up in every way into him who is the head, into Christ" (Ephesians 4:15). Anyone embarking on a journey with Christ will be changed by that journey. If this is not in the mind as well as the heart, the process will not be complete. The question that should be asked is whether we are willing to have a deeper relationship with Christ and know his truth as we walk with him.

In the late 1950s the winds of change were blowing away the old world order of colonialism. African and Asian people were taking on responsibility for running their own countries and taking control of their own destiny. Max Warren, then head of the Church Missionary Society, began to reflect on the implications for mission, ministry, and theology. The assumption of the traditional missionary was that the Church of England was the repository of truth and that missionaries could teach "natives" how to be Christian. The faith they proclaimed was based on the Bible as understood through a European cultural lens. The struggle for independence challenged such paternalist notions. In its place Warren proposed partnership—a relationship of mutuality. In this context, Warren argued, it was impossible to understand any one culture holding all truth, and he uttered the revolutionary words "only the whole world knows the whole truth."[5]

A similar change took place in North America. Most of the missionary work with Indigenous peoples involved practices that disvalued and destroyed their cultures in favor of those rooted in European tradition. Both The Episcopal Church and the Anglican Church of Canada began a journey during the 1960s that led to a new understanding of mission as a mutual and interdependent relationship, and which has led to steps being taken in support of the cultural and spiritual recovery of Indigenous peoples.

The search for truth is a dialogue between companions on a journey. As we share perspectives, we discover more and more as we learn from one another.

Continuing Indaba journeys

In 2010 the twelve diocesan teams from across the Anglican Communion set out on the Continuing Indaba journeys described in the Introduction. Each diocese had a team of eight, and every person came into the experience differently. Some were sure they had both truth and clarity; all they needed, they thought, was to explain well and their view would prevail. Others came into the experience feeling vulnerable, quite sure that their experience and voice would not be heard. During the encounters, the teams worshiped, traveled and ate together. Some understood the journey as a pilgrimage and, like a pilgrimage, the aim was to discover a deeper relationship with Christ. They visited many church projects and were eager to learn about the context of each diocese, but real significance was found in the relationships that were formed.

Initially there was an eagerness to address problems and not to "waste time." But in hindsight, the teams valued the time to establish relationships so that they could recognize Christ in one another before moving to genuine conversation. The relationships formed on the journey created the space for truth to be spoken and heard, with all seeking to hear God rather than to win an argument. The conversations were not easy, but participants shared their anxieties and fears, together with their hopes and joys.

Frankie Lee, from the Hong Kong team, describes the challenging blessing of building and sustaining relationship with members of the dioceses of Jamaica and Toronto, as well as from the Province of Hong Kong:

> I treasure very much the friendship and company of my fellow Indaba members. We sometimes hold very different views from each other, but there is trust among us. We believe in each other. We know that all of us care about the Church, about the Communion, about God's mission, and, therefore, we are willing to listen. There is willingness among

us not only to listen, but to be challenged, even to be changed by the "other." I believe this is what Christian journey is all about—going into the unknown, not knowing where the conversation will lead us or where we will end up being, yet trusting totally in the Spirit to guide us.[6]

Frankie describes here the need to live out an uncertain journey. This is something we are all called to do in order to Live Reconciliation. There is a whole world of diversity in our churches and communities—we do not need to travel far to find it. In terms of present geography, Peter's physical journey following Jesus was relatively short. During the life of Christ, he only traveled the kinds of distances we consider possible in a day by car, and during his lifetime only distances that would be a week's vacation on a cruise ship. The distance was not important; the journey was.

This is not a journey we take alone. The starting point is to value the people we are traveling with. The global issues of violence we see in the news become irreconcilable when the protagonists themselves see the issues in black and white. When there are two opposing factions trying to gain or keep power, they lose any sense of being able to love their neighbors without forcing them to be like themselves. Reconciliation begins when we stop seeing other people as enemies and protagonists, and start to see them as friends on a common journey.

Living Reconciliation is about being prepared to listen and to speak. This can mean a whole attitude change in how we approach discussion. Even people from the same culture communicate differently. Some people are very quick to speak and can dominate group discussions. Others need time to form their thoughts. Some people analyze the world and value reason and structure, while others find their instinct and intuition are more reliable. We also are shaped by our experiences, and these can affect the way we think.

Building relationships and learning about one another's context are vital to begin to understand how to genuinely hear one another. It is sometimes easier to have feelings of affection for people whom we know at a distance. Their faults are hidden from us. Distant friends may not understand why a sister is angry with her brother, for example. It is also easier to hate someone we stereotype so long as we don't know them. Authentic and mutual listening has to be grounded in relationships so that it can get beyond a superficial level.

The first step in Living Reconciliation is to start on a journey. The next is to recognize that this is a journey with companions. This is different from journeying to a foreign land with friends from your own place. It is leaving your own place and joining with companions who are different from you on a journey together into uncertainty.

* * *

Prayer

> Loving God, author of truth,
> sustain us as we journey into uncertainty
> and together enter deeper into your Story.
> *Amen.*

Questions to think about

1. Who do you see as your neighbor? Does this put limits on those to whom you show love?

2. How do you engage with those whose lives and ways confuse or intimidate you?

3. When have you encountered something you assume to be true that was questioned by someone you trust? How did you react?

Further thinking

For additional material on the topics discussed in this chapter—including videos, study guides, and further reading—please visit www.living-reconciliation.org.

Chapter 3

Companions

Living reconciliation is a journey with companions, and you cannot choose those you travel with. It also requires moving out from the normal boundaries that fence in your world and encountering people you would not normally get to know. Discovering new places and new people, experiencing new tastes and new songs, is exciting—it is how many of us spend our vacations. But in the end, people tend to return to friends and communities that share common values.

It's often said that in church we make friends with people whom we never would come to know otherwise. This is a sign of an outward-looking church. Inward-looking churches are resistant to outsiders. They welcome those who like the music and the style of worship. They welcome people who share the values of the inner circle and who don't rock the boat. They can be reluctant to change when new people bring in new ideas and ways.

The rector of a smart church in a rural town became aware of the plight of immigrant workers harvesting crops for low pay and suffering under difficult conditions. They were far from home and spoke a different language. They were trying hard to improve their life and offer hope for their families. He listened to them and offered them practical assistance. Some began to come to the Sunday morning worship. Not long after, a leading member whose family had worshiped at the church for many years quietly told the rector, "we only want to worship on Sunday with people we would be happy to party with on Saturday night. Don't try to make us uncomfortable." He was very happy for the rector to add an alternative service at another time for the migrants, but he did not want to mix with people of a different social standing.

Living Reconciliation is uncomfortable. It begins with the understanding that the love of God is for all people, not just those who are like us. Just how different people can be is a shock; it was to the community who followed Jesus. This chapter will look at the significance, challenges, and joys of crossing cultures, and will consider the skills required to be open to understanding that "only the whole world knows the whole truth."[1]

Community in the followers of Jesus

When Peter set out on his journey with Jesus, he was with people like himself. Peter and his brother Andrew were partners in a fishing business with James and John, and they may very well have known one another all their lives. They were not identical in character or temperament but they had the same background, laughed at the same jokes, sang the same songs, and ate the same foods. They shared a common culture.

As businessmen, they would most certainly have had similar and hostile feelings about tax collectors, so when Jesus calls Levi (also known as Matthew) as his disciple, there would have been some initial discomfort.[2] The fishermen would have felt hounded by this tax collector, probably seeing him as a corrupt lackey of an oppressive regime. The tax collector may likewise have viewed the fishermen as dishonest men trying to avoid paying what was due. And this involves only five of twelve men!

Of course the twelve were not the only followers in Jesus' community. We know there were women as well, and Luke's Gospel speaks of seventy-two disciples sent out on a mission. Jesus had drawn to himself a group of followers who at the very beginning had to cross cultural barriers in order to work out what reconciliation meant in practice. Trust would have to be built and cultural assumptions and stereotypes would have to be broken down. All these men and women had in common was the fact that when Jesus said "Follow me," they left everything behind and followed.

In October 2011, as part of their Continuing Indaba journey, the Diocese of El Camino Real in California welcomed teams of eight from the Dioceses of Western Tanganyika (Tanzania) and Gloucester (England) to its diocesan convention, part of The Episcopal Church's form of governance. The visiting teams were meeting up with the team of eight from California for the first time since they had traveled for ten days together in western Tanzania earlier that year. The initial partnership between the bishops had moved into a growing relationship between dioceses, with lay and ordained people involved. In 2010 they had formally joined the pilot program of Continuing Indaba.

Bishop Sadock Makaya, the newly elected Bishop of Western Tanganyika, had a great advantage in joining the Continuing Indaba team—he had crossed cultural barriers before. During a sermon to the convention, he recounted an incident on his first visit to the United States when he was offered a hot dog. His desire to please his hosts was met by his internal revulsion at the very idea, and he replied, as politely as he could, "In my country, we do not eat dogs." He told this story at the convention's opening service, not only to raise a laugh but also to encourage others to explore the effort required to cross cultures.

The first Continuing Indaba journey made by the teams from Mumbai (India) and Derby (England) was to the Diocese of

New York. On the first day, there was an opportunity for the twenty-four team members to visit St. Paul's Chapel, which had been under the shadow of the twin towers of the World Trade Center since they were erected in the 1970s. On September 11, 2001, St. Paul's was used as a makeshift support center for firefighters, police, and construction workers, offering a place of rest and recovery in the immediate aftermath of the collapse of the buildings. It continued in that role for a further eight months. St. Paul's now is a working chapel but it carries the reminders of those difficult days, including words and mementos from people around the world expressing their grief and sympathy.

Emerging into the sunlight and overlooking Ground Zero, the team gathered to pray. As they did so, the Bishop of Mumbai recalled the attack on his home city by Lashkar-e-Taiba in 2008 and reminded the Derby team of the July 7 bombings in London in 2005. Tears flowed as they prayed, and a bond was formed that cut across their divides. Each team was bound by the commitment to oppose terrorism in any form. That evening, following evensong, the dean of the Cathedral of St. John the Divine addressed the group. He spoke with eloquence of the change that had been affected in the psyche and culture of New York since the fall of the twin towers. He spoke of a sense of oneness and a breaking down of cultural barriers in the city. He said that people now spoke to one another on the subway and challenged bad behavior. There was no glorification of the disaster, but a sense that in New York the commitment had been made to live a better way.

One member of the New York team was quiet. Winnie Varghese is a priest in the Diocese of New York and her experience of the time after 9/11 was different from her companions. As a South Indian, her looks singled her out for many New Yorkers as being like the terrorists. Her experience was of the majority of New Yorkers closing ranks against any people who looked as if they might be a Muslim. Her experience of 9/11 was not heroic; it was the pretext for prejudice to grow. She felt judged, isolated, and outside the warm feelings of companionship that others had experienced.

Relationships are complex matters and the sense of a common bond between some can, at the same time, isolate others. A bond had formed between all kinds of New Yorkers, but those who looked "Muslim" were outside that bond. They were made aware they were the strangers, even if they were Christian ministers.

The diversity encountered during the Continuing Indaba journeys might seem extreme. However, many dioceses have this kind of diversity, and the experience of culture can change by just crossing a street. This diversity is a strength if it is faced and owned. It is a weakness if congregations withdraw into their own safe ground and try to ignore all others around them. If our church is going to grow, we need to step out of our comfort zone and cross barriers. Only then can we understand the partnerships we have with those around us.

Every now and then it is important for Christians to read all of a gospel in one sitting. We are used to getting snippets read to us in services. We hear a few verses one week and then another section a week later. Many of us use Bible devotions or notes. These daily readings chop up the Bible into small sections for us to digest. Reading the whole story from beginning to end is a quite different experience.

Many years ago a British actor recited Mark's Gospel in a one-man show that toured the United Kingdom. To the surprise of all, he performed the gospel word for word to sell-out audiences. The effect was electrifying, and it probably replicated how Mark intended the gospel to be heard. If you try this yourself—find a quiet space and just read it aloud—you will see the text in a whole new light.

You will find in the first eight chapters of Mark's Gospel that there is a lot of wandering around, seemingly aimlessly. In these opening chapters, Jesus seems to be crossing the lake backward and forward in an almost random way. However, the movement is not random; it signifies a transition from Jewish to Gentile areas. The Gentile areas are marked by such things as the presence of pig farms. Mark records Jesus' encounters with various women and men, and with some who would not have shared the same world-views as Jesus and his close companions. This is a journey into a conversation with those who were not only different in their outward appearance: they thought differently, ate differently, laughed at different jokes, and worshiped in different ways and in different places.

John's Gospel records the same kind of movement, the same crossing of cultural barriers, and the same sense of wandering until Jesus marches into Jerusalem. One encounter stands out above all others: the encounter at the well with a Samaritan woman.

Jesus and the Samaritan woman

To our modern outsider eyes, the Samaritans that Jesus would have encountered as he and his disciples took the unconventional route through Samaria from Judea to Galilee would not have seemed very different. The Samaritans and the Israelites came from the same root; they both saw themselves as descendants of Abraham and received the same laws from Moses. When, after the death of Solomon, the twelve tribes of Israel divided into the Northern and Southern Kingdoms, the people who came to be known as the Samaritans developed separately from the Jews. By the time of Jesus, these two peoples had a long adversarial history, each considering the other to have deviated drastically from the ancient faith of Israel.

When Jesus and the Samaritan woman meet at Jacob's well—a shared place of significance in all the Abrahamic faiths—the social, religious, and political enmity between their people gives rise to a palpable tension in the air. Though unnamed in scripture, the Eastern Orthodox tradition names this woman Photine, meaning "light," and celebrates her as a saint and martyr.

When Jesus asked Photine for a drink, he is breaking many taboos. For a Jew to address a Samaritan man would have been troublesome, but for a man alone to talk to a woman was culturally unacceptable. Jews considered Samaritans to be unclean; in asking Photine to give him a drink from her drinking vessel, Jesus is breaking Jewish law. Jesus is also initiating a risky conversation. He steps out of the comfort zone of his tradition, and in doing so invites her to do likewise. Photine's response is to challenge Jesus on his motives.[3]

When we begin to Live Reconciliation we find ourselves mimicking the dance of Jesus and Photine. We may become more and more aware of the baggage of cultural stereotypes and morality judgments, both of ourselves and our companions. Like Photine we may keep a barrier between ourselves and our companions because it is easier and feels safer than engaging with and unpacking this baggage together.

Jesus invites Photine to go deeper into conversation by asking her to see him as he is, beyond the stereotypes she has of Jewish men, and he draws out of her more about herself—who she is—beyond "just" being a Samaritan woman. Their dialogue is important as Jesus reveals some of himself and speaks to her of who she is. As their conversation goes deeper, it comes back to the historical enmity between their two peoples. Photine's question hits at the very heart of the conflict between

Samaritans and Jews when she asks, "Where is the correct center of worship?" For Jews it is Mount Zion, and for Samaritans it is Mount Gerazim; it would be impossible for there to be a compromise solution, as one or other must be right.

Their conversation up to this point, though not an easy one, has created a safe space between them; and so Photine is able to raise this uncomfortable question knowing that the wrong answer could end all further conversation. Jesus' answer is surprising and leads to him revealing that he is the promised Messiah. Photine, a Samaritan, is the first in John's Gospel to hear Jesus claiming this title for himself.

When we make the commitment to engage in Living Reconciliation, we have to open ourselves up to conversations such as the one between Jesus and Photine. We need the courage to put aside stereotypes of others and of ourselves, and to explore our faith and contexts together. We cannot go cold into difficult conversations without ending up polarizing one another. In this encounter Jesus and Photine begin by working through their cultural baggage, to a place where they are able to acknowledge each other, and then to a safe place for Photine to ask a difficult and risky question that goes to the heart of what separates their two communities. In Living Reconciliation we need to be able to engage with the baggage that separates us—not just to decide on what we agree or disagree—but to be able to get to the point where we can recognize one another as followers of Christ on a journey. It is then, once we have formed a relationship based on a shared bond with Christ and made a safe space to talk, that we can come back to what separates us as part of a shared journey.

When the disciples return with the food they have bought, John tells us that they are utterly astonished to see Jesus in conversation with Photine. The appearance of Peter and the other disciples, just as Jesus is revealing his identity as the Messiah, is Photine's cue to begin a new part of her journey— one that draws her whole village into an encounter with Jesus. In the same way, when a few companions from different contexts set out to journey together with one another and with Christ, whole communities can be drawn in.

Just as Jesus' conversation with the Samaritan woman was counter-cultural, so was the disciples' shopping trip. For a Jew to buy from a Samaritan and a Samaritan to sell to a Jew was not a common or accepted practice. When the disciples return, John tells us they were astonished. This is not a passing shock but an ongoing amazement at Jesus' actions.[4] Jesus calls all his disciples to go beyond their own boundaries, cultural expectations, and even beliefs, so they can come to Live Reconciliation.

Crossing cultures

Just as Jesus went on a cross-cultural journey with his disciples, we too must engage in a cross-cultural journey to Live Reconciliation. This is both harder and easier than it sounds.

While we don't need to travel great distances, we are required to develop skills, and this may demand hard work. The teams on the Continuing Indaba journey found that they had the opportunity to take seriously the cultures of those they were journeying with from around the world, and in doing so they formed the skills to Live Reconciliation locally.

Ken Wratten was a member of the team from the Diocese of El Camino Real. He was weary of the long confrontation between liberals and conservatives in his own church. As someone identified as a "conservative," he had seen many friends leave his church, and he was expecting more confrontation. After completing the journey he wrote:

> All of us quickly realized that the opportunity being offered in the Indaba experience was to reject our urge to defend a position, but to simply befriend the people, visit their homes, meet their children, eat their food, visit their churches, experience their efforts in evangelism and discipleship, and then to discuss the significant issues we face together as the people of God.
>
> Through the course of our talks, the definition of "poverty" became much more multi-dimensional; the western weakness in evangelism was glaring; the importance of ANY labels relating to color, wealth of resources,

sexuality, or conservative versus liberal theology became increasingly secondary. By the end of our Indaba conversations at Pilgrim Hall in early March 2012, there was a palpable sense within our group of twenty-four that we had really become one in Christ, committed to continuing conversations and working together for the purpose of helping each other more effectively be the Body of Christ. And this wasn't just talk. We left with some programs defined, and more in the queue.[5]

Ken had moved from seeking to defend a position to one of valuing diversity. Defense is a common reaction from individuals and groups who believe that their way of seeing the world is the only viable one. It can happen when dominant groups see minorities as a threat and when minority groups defend themselves by stressing a closed identity and sense of belonging. In our churches this can become very destructive. For Ken it was a relief to go beyond defending a position to discovering value in all and being valued himself.

What Ken found was acceptance. He was valued for who he was and what he believed and not marginalized for holding a minority opinion within his diocese. The diversity of cultures across the groups turned out to be part of accepting the diversity within them. Tensions might exist, but they are healthy if they are kept in dialogue on the way to the search for truth.

When we become locked into polarized debates, we become convinced that there must be one answer or another that is "true." For the Jews and Samaritans, it was the true place of worship, Zion or Gerazim. Jesus does not dismiss the passion of either, but changes the debate. The truth is not in a location, but it is in the relationship with God through the Spirit that is open to all.

When communities or individuals engage, some are tempted to iron out differences, to stress that we all really believe the same thing, and that we are much the same. This is not true. When the Spirit came upon Peter and his companions at Pentecost, the people were not given the gift of understanding the one language of heaven. The preachers were given the gift to speak in many languages. The good news of Jesus was translated into numerous cultural dialects, each one with its own nuances and emphases. There is value in our differences.

Another story from another journey illustrates the same point from a very different perspective. Kevin, a gay member of the Hong Kong team, was not able to come out easily in his home culture. He reflected at the end of the Indaba that his mind-set had been "rather narrow," he would befriend those who shared similar values to him, and those with whom he could feel safe being himself. It was around the meal tables of Hong Kong that he began to reach out and it was in Jamaica, and with Jamaican Christians who hold very different understandings of sexuality, that he was able to come out. He could do so because he was among friends who accepted him, even if they had not changed their minds. Reflecting on his experience, Kevin wrote that it was after they had "built up good relationships during Indaba" that they were able to "truly acknowledge and respect the differences among us without seeking to 'change' the other."

Ken and Kevin have never met. They participated in very different journeys, but they both experienced the difficulties of defending a minority conviction in their own church. They were both enriched by the cross-cultural journey on the way to accepting and being accepted. They have not changed their minds nor do they minimize the differences they face. Kevin speaks of no longer being on a side fighting across a barrier, but being in a boat on a common journey with people who disagree with you but who are still part of the same community.

Forming journeying communities

A theological educator in another country sent his students to place a bet in a local bookmaking parlor. He was not hoping to addict them to gambling but to send them to one of the more uncomfortable places possible. He did so to force them to cross a cultural barrier and learn what it was to feel in an unsafe space. For many regulars placing their bets, it was a place of safety; but ask them to church and they would panic. If these future clergy were not able to understand this discomfort, they would never be effective.

On a journey together, it is often useful to come to a place where all are uncomfortable in order for a genuine conversation to emerge. Gaining a depth of understanding does not come quickly or easily; it requires a commitment of time and openness to vulnerability. It means sharing in one another's places of comfort and also understanding that, for the visitor, it can be a very threatening environment. This is why staying in one another's homes, shopping, going out for a drink or a meal, or watching sports with others from different contexts can be so important. It also means entering into a place that might be safe for your companion, but might be very scary for you.

For Christians, worshiping together in spirit and truth is a crucial part of the journey. This may mean worshiping in a completely different style from that which is familiar. Being able to worship with and recognize the Christian journey of our companions was one of the most powerful experiences described by the participants in the Continuing Indaba pilot program. Along with this comes sharing our own mission situation and discovering how all those on the journey seek to serve God in their own circumstances.

The journey requires a great deal of dedicated time set aside to be with one another, honoring that time, and sticking to the commitment decided at the beginning. It requires vulnerability and honesty to share our own context in a genuine way. It also requires being open to listening and being inquisitive about our companions' mission setting without being judgmental or comparing it, negatively or positively, to our own. When we begin building communities that are journeying together, we become part of one another's stories.

New York is a place of extremes. It has great wealth, and it has absolute poverty. It is very rural and very urban. The diocese has important questions to ask about its future in mission, as do all dioceses. The "can do" culture of New York leads to the expectation that there are instant solutions to any problem. In 2013 the incoming Bishop of New York was faced with big problems. Some were calling for smaller churches to be closed, and others feared it would be their churches facing the cut. The new bishop did something counter-cultural; he rejected the quick fix and sent the diocese on a journey, an Indaba journey. He asked members to enter into a planned and facilitated program of parishes visiting one another across the diocese. In the first round, nearly a third of the parishes participated, forming teams to visit and encounter one another's setting. The bishop also demanded a high level of commitment. They were to spend the best part of two days in their partner parishes. They were to stay the night, hosted by members of the congregation and not in hotels, and they were to pray for one another. It could be deeply intimidating for all concerned, but the bishop could see no other way to develop a common understanding of their spiritual life. They had no other way of realistically considering how they could go forward in mission together. The only answer was a journey that crossed cultures.

Welcoming the representatives—four from each parish—Bishop Andrew Deitsche called on them to enter into a spiritual as well as a physical journey to develop a shared understanding of their common life as a diocese. At the diocesan convention later that year, the bishop, in his address, described a conversation he had following the first encounter weekend:

> A member of one of our significant Manhattan churches, in partnership with a small church upstate and a congregation in the Bronx, told me that by the end of the weekend everyone was crying. She said that this has changed her life. It has changed her understanding of church. She told me these things from a heart welling over with feeling. And I confess that the passion of some of these reports has taken me aback. What have I done, I wondered; I've started something and I don't know where it's going. But later she came back to me and said, "You know, Bishop Dietsche, this Indaba has an unintended consequence for you!" And when I asked what that is, she said that if we go to close one of those smaller or poorer churches, we need to know that "they are our friends now!" And I laughed and said that that was the whole point. It is this which I have prayed for this diocese: the beginning of A

Shared Understanding of Our Common Life;
it is the beginning of Everybody All Together,
Everybody Being One.[6]

This is what it means to begin to share a Living Reconciliation journey—to begin to understand one another as journeying with Christ, even if there are more differences than similarities. The implications of the Indaba journey were only beginning to be understood by the Diocese of New York. They have begun to dismantle barriers that divide them into rich and poor or into "strong" and "weak." They still have tough choices to make, but now the answers can emerge from a shared vision and respect. Choices can be considered and not rushed into, and they can result in mission outcomes, not those determined only by finance.

Beyond respect

It is easy to talk about valuing diversity but much more difficult to live it out. When we celebrate Holy Eucharist, we remember that "Though we are many we are one body." Taking these words seriously is both a joyful and a painful journey. If we are all one, we share one another's sufferings as well as celebrate one another's joys. If one part of the body hurts, we all hurt. When we celebrate, we all celebrate. The aim of Living Reconciliation is to go beyond seeing a person as different, and to see him or her simply as another human being. It does not take away difference, but enables us to see that we are incomplete in our individuality; we are whole in community. Africans have many proverbs that express this belief. The most simple is the Swahili phrase "Mtu ni watu," which literally translated means "a person is people."

However, there is a consequence. If all are equal, we begin to question the power structures that define our churches and our world. These structures define some as more important than others. Jesus challenges these power structures, and his embrace of the notion of servant leadership revolutionizes the way we see the world.

* * *

Prayer

> Loving God, you desire your people to be
> one as you are One. Teach us that oneness in
> your likeness is full of the joy of diversity. We
> ask this in your name, Father, Son, and Holy
> Spirit. *Amen.*

Questions to think about

1. When have you come up against stereotypes, either of you or your stereotypes of others? How did you work through them?

2. When have you experienced conversations like the one Jesus and Photine had at the well? What did you learn about yourself and the other person?

3. We often say that we value diversity. What does it mean to you for the church to be the diverse people of God together?

Further thinking

For additional material on the topics discussed in this chapter—including videos, study guides, and further reading—please visit www.living-reconciliation.org.

Chapter 4

Encounter with power

Throughout this book, we are consciously celebrating the diversity of the world we live in. As human beings, many of us love crossing cultures. Just consider how much money is spent on vacations seeking out authentic local tastes and sounds. Sometimes we don't need to travel very far. In the great cities of the world there are areas where people of different cultures congregate. Take, for example, the Chinatowns of London, Singapore, San Francisco, and Vancouver. These are thriving and engaging places that draw all sorts of people to enjoy the food, shop, and experience a different culture—especially around the time of the lunar New Year. In reality all our cities are marked by distinctive areas. This can be a wonderful part of life, except when these areas come to define inequality marked by social and economic exclusion.

If we are Living Reconciliation, we cannot ignore injustice when the barriers that divide are marked by inequality of status, power, and wealth. Breaking down the barriers is not about ending diversity; it is about valuing all, and inequality of status is one of the biggest barriers to overcome. In order for barriers to be challenged, there is a need to confront the power structures that hold them in place.

Throughout the centuries many political systems have been founded along ethnic lines, building up barriers based on difference. The biblical narrative of Egyptians enslaving the people of Israel captures this, and has had deep resonances for those escaping slavery throughout the ages. Economic systems grew out of the exploitation of enslaved people and the limiting opportunities of racial and ethnic segregation, supported by beliefs among many in the dominant group that this type of inequality was morally and religiously acceptable. In the Victorian era, a strain of English Christianity believed that some were born to be wealthy and powerful and others to serve them. This was encapsulated in the hymn, "All things bright and beautiful." The original third verse reads:

> The rich man in his castle,
> The poor man at his gate,
> God made them high and lowly,
> And ordered their estate.

We may never sing these lines, but these orders of society are still too identifiable today.

In the nineteenth and twentieth centuries, two stark statements stood out on the ideology of building barriers: the Jim Crow segregation laws in the United States and the apartheid system in South Africa. African Americans who had been enslaved were protected following the Civil War by federal civil rights laws. But after federal troops were withdrawn from the South, conservative white politicians enacted laws state by state that, from the 1880s until the mid-1960s, rigidly segregated black and white people. Segregation meant inferior housing, schools, services, and work opportunities including the daily humiliation of being unable to use the same seats in buses or cafes, or the same restrooms and drinking fountains, as white people. Most churches were segregated as well. Although little in Christian theology could justify segregation, prejudice and racism were deeply embedded within the white majority.

Apartheid in South Africa institutionalized divisions defined by ethnicity and argued that it was good and ordained by God. It is hard for most of us who did not live in South Africa in the apartheid years to understand how significant the theological arguments were to those who ran the country. Theologians taught a theology that underpinned the injustice and claimed that the Bible itself established the division of the races. People were kept apart under the notion that the Bible demanded that distinctive races shouldn't mix, with the white race claiming the ability to rule over all others, especially black Africans.

The world rejoiced when both of these regimes came to an end. A key part of the wide-ranging Civil Rights movement, the Rev. Dr. Martin Luther King Jr., and a large coalition of black church leaders and their members acted to bring about racial justice and equality, grounded in a biblical and Christian understanding of freedom and inclusion. Their efforts were also joined by white Christians, Jews, and others during the 1960s. Rev. Dr. King put forth his powerful vision of racial reconciliation in his "I Have a Dream" speech given at the 1963 March on Washington, a year before the Civil Rights Act was signed into law.

In South Africa apartheid came to an end in 1994 with the first democratic elections. The theology of reconciliation and justice was embraced and a commitment was given to the poor and the oppressed. The false gospel of division was at an end, and it was time to celebrate. However, the destruction of one legal system is not the end of all such divisions. Segregation and apartheid may sound like the extreme, but structures in every society play on racial and ethnic divisions to create inequality. Too often there is some very well thought out reason why one group should retain power and marginalize others.

One of the most significant powers for a human being is to be able to speak for oneself, and not to be spoken for. The opening of the United States Declaration of Independence, written in 1776, declares that "all men are created equal." However, it was nearly a hundred years later that President Abraham Lincoln applied this to slaves and only in 1920 that women gained the equal right to vote. Not until 1965 were Indigenous Americans assured the right to vote.[1] With no right to vote, there was no power to speak, and decisions were made for most of the population without their active involvement.

Even today many people are excluded from decision-making processes that determine how they can live. Marginalized people sometimes seek advocates to speak on their behalf. But, as we saw in chapter 2, advocacy is limited in its effectiveness. Speaking on behalf of those who do not have a voice can be an important and prophetic role. However, it does suggest that a particular group needs someone to speak for them, as if their voice is not acceptable or they are not capable. The voice, and the control of that voice, remains with those who have power. Even if this power is benevolent, it is still belittling as it does not share power with those who are marginalized.

Consider your reaction to this quote from the great German theologian Paul Tillich as he explores the relationship between justice and listening in his book *Love, Power, and Justice*:

> In order to know what is just in a person-to-person encounter love listens. It is its first task to listen. No human relation, especially no intimate one, is possible without mutual listening...[All People] call on us with small or loud voices. They want us to listen, they want us to understand their intrinsic claims, their justice of being. They want justice from us. But we can give it to them only through the love which listens...Listening Love is the first step to justice in person-to-person encounters.[2]

At first glance this is inspirational. We are called to listen and build relationships as we discover that listening love is the first step to justice. But Tillich's understanding is ultimately limiting. He understands that it is the work of the powerful to listen to the powerless and to offer love. He also understands justice as something "given." Justice that is the gift of the powerful to the weak is not justice at all. Justice is a not a judgment; it is living in freedom. Justice is for all or it is not justice.

Living Reconciliation requires mutual listening and requires a further step to the point where the very notions of power are understood in a completely different way. This chapter will explore how Living Reconciliation challenges our very notions of the "natural order" of society. This is based in the essence of Jesus' Incarnation. In Jesus, God is made known to us in the life of a human being who held little social status— born in a stable, living in poverty, and dying by torture. This act revolutionizes how we look at the world.

Jesus, Lord, King, and Messiah

When Jesus met Pilate, he was introduced as one who was claiming to be king. He did not directly deny the accusation, but he redefined it. Pilate believed he knew what power was. If he sent out an order, it was to be obeyed. If he demanded payment, he was paid. Power was the ability to command another person's life. Great power was to command the lives of many people, and to have one's own life commanded by few or none. To confront this power Jesus would need an army, and Jesus did not have an army.

One common response to unjust power is revolution: when those who are oppressed rise up in the hope of overthrowing those people and structures that have exploited them. However, this rarely leads to shared and equal power. The new order often replicates the old, with new people in power using repression to maintain their own version of the same story.

What marks the great reconcilers is not only their stand against oppression, but also their deep commitment to ending vicious circles of revenge. Among those who gave their lives for such a cause was the Archbishop of Uganda, Janani Luwum, whose statue is among those over the west door of Westminster Abbey, honoring martyrs of the twentieth century.

Archbishop Luwum led the protest against the brutal dictator Idi Amin in the 1970s. He did not call for violence to be responded to with violence, but led a peaceful response. In 1977 he was murdered and the protest became international. Among Archbishop Luwum's closest friends openly protesting at the reign of terror in their land was Bishop Festo Kivengere, an evangelist who had brought life to the Anglican Church of Tanzania in the 1950s and who was later known as a companion to Billy Graham.

Bishop Kivengere had escaped from Uganda just a month before the murder of his friend. He shocked many people by publishing a book with the provocative title, *I Love Idi Amin*.

He was well aware that such a statement could be viewed as a Christian cliché. One day when he was faced by someone accusing him of hesitating to condemn the vile dictator, he said, "My ministry is not the ministry of condemnation. My ministry is the ministry of reconciliation."[3]

The words did not come easily to the bishop. He attributed them at the time to the Holy Spirit. The accuser then asked him a question that put him on the spot, and this is his own account of the encounter:

> He said, "Supposing I brought Amin and made him stand there in front of you and I gave you a pistol. Tell me, what would you do with that pistol?"
>
> That was a little bit tough, but I said to him, "Look, I would hand over the gun to Amin, saying, 'Take your weapon, it belongs to you. I've never used it, I don't believe in it. My only weapon is love.'"
>
> I love Idi Amin because by not loving him my protest would have failed.[4]

Bishop Kivengere was imitating Jesus, who when standing in front of Pilate had rejected the way of force and looked to a different understanding of power.

The idea of servant leadership may seem very familiar. We may sing songs that celebrate it, such as "The Servant King," and listen to sermons exulting it, but we rarely grasp just how big a change it means to live as followers of Jesus. Emptying himself of power was the most challenging thing Jesus did. In imitating Christ our next task is to consider how challenging this is for us.

Jesus meets the power question

It was not just in his encounter with Pilate that Jesus confronted power. Throughout the gospels we find Jesus taking on either the religious and state authorities or the destructive power of demons. So it comes as a bit of a surprise in Mark 7:24–30 when it is Jesus who is challenged about his own use of power. In the previous passage we find Jesus challenging some pharisees and scribes in Jerusalem on their interpretation of tradition to suit themselves and oppress others.

Following this encounter Jesus sets out for Tyre, a Gentile town. There he encounters a Syro-Phoenician woman, whom tradition calls Justa. She seeks Jesus' help for her daughter. When the woman approaches Jesus, begging him to heal her little girl, his first response was to silence her. In telling her that it is not right to give the children's bread to the dogs he is telling her that she had no access to him because of who she was. This is shocking. Jesus is telling her that because he is the Jewish Messiah, she as a Gentile—a foreigner—has no access to God's healing for her daughter through him.

What is more shocking is that, although powerless, she is able to speak to Jesus. The desperate mother has nothing to lose and so challenges Jesus' position and his power as a Jewish man, breaking down his traditional assumptions and barriers.

There are many times in church when young people, women, or those who are on the edges are silenced by authority and power—authoritative voices that say "You do not get to ask that question" or, "The decision has been made; you have no voice here." This is in effect what Jesus is saying to the unnamed mother—"The decision about who gets to experience my power has already been made." The woman's retort is harsh.

Then comes the moment of beauty in the tale. Jesus does not storm off or use his power to oppress the woman. He does as she asks. We do not find here, as in other healing tales, Jesus' words telling the supplicant that their faith has healed them. Here Jesus tells her that "because you have said that"— "because you have recognized who I am and have challenged my power and challenged me to think about my power—then your daughter is healed."

The meeting between Jesus and Justa, the Syro-Phoenician mother, is a radical moment in Mark's Gospel. Jesus is challenged to see his power and his mission in a wider context. In his life and teaching, Jesus continues to redefine and challenge power. Anyone described as king, messiah, or lord is expected to exert dominating power, to take control, and rule. The "King of the Jews" who faced Pilate confounded any such classification. Right from his conception, through his life and especially in his death, Jesus challenged that idea.

Reconciliation is only possible if we embrace Jesus' way of how we live individually and in community. When we engage in Living Reconciliation, power, and authority—assumed and real, used and abused—are things that need to be acknowledged, challenged, and shared. This path is incredibly difficult, and we may find ourselves being dragged back into ways of behaving that replicate this dominating power and returning to ways that deny Jesus' witness of humility and service.

Power and leadership

The hierarchies in our society are frequently reflected in our churches. Some people may be considered more important than others and given greater honor. They may have that honor because of the years they have been coming to church, their particular talents, their education, or their wealth. Sometimes these power structures play out in very subtle ways, but sometimes they are obvious to all. The most significant is the way we treat clergy and laity.

Clergy are rarely reticent. At the launch event of the New York diocesan Indaba, the sixty-four participants were split into teams of twelve. Sitting at circular tables in the nave of the cathedral, they were asked to talk about their hopes and fears for the Indaba journey ahead of them. Observers mingled, moving from table to table picking up themes, which they later reported back. What they all found was that the clergy spoke up loudly, assumed the role of chairing the discussion, and took control. Lay people were sometimes hard to hear and sometimes reticent to speak, even in a place like New York. If confronted, the clergy would be shocked. They might never intend to exert power, but in a church setting it is difficult to avoid.

Put a bishop with clergy and the dynamic changes again. The clergy now have a person who may judge them and their suitability for finding a new role or placement. The power of a recommendation made or withheld can make or break new opportunities. This is made explicit for example in the Church of England where "preferment" is the word used for someone moving to a "senior" position. They are preferred over others and reliant on those in power knowing them and thinking highly of them. Although many senior positions in The Episcopal Church are filled through an open search process, most clergy are aware of the power of informal networks to support or hinder their prospects.

But when clergy are wary of rocking the boat, lay people may come to the fore to speak more easily. Articulate and influential lay people also can speak up and confront a bishop who has no power over them. If they hold the key to funding they hold power over bishops, who are aware of the financial implications if they are offended. All of these examples show problematic uses of power—clergy who routinely assume the leadership of an open conversation, and anyone who exerts power to create dependency in others for the security of their own position or ministry.

Some people of great influence and power in their own culture participated in the Indaba journeys. We had a university professor, a wealthy and influential business person, a head teacher, and a doctor. Some were key people in their diocese who spoke with confidence. Other lay people were used to being spoken for. They were not powerful in the world's eyes but they were frequently active in transforming their own societies. They were young and old, women and men; they were often the servant leaders and outstanding evangelists, and they were the people who could often speak of their involvement in challenging injustice. All these people needed to find a voice without silencing others.

Living Reconciliation requires that all be able to speak and listen. The issue of power came to the fore early in one of the Indaba journeys. The groups agreed to meet to discuss three issues of significance outlined by their bishops. The bishops were present, and presentations were prepared. One member of each team spoke, and then there was a general discussion chaired by people who were respected by all. Among the group of twenty-four, the three bishops made over fifty percent of the comments, and they were rarely challenged. Some people, lay and ordained, said nothing at all over three long meetings. People would signal to those chairing that they wished to speak, but the bishops did not notice and spoke without waiting to be called by the chair. It was not that they were being rude, they genuinely did not notice; and because they were bishops, no one challenged them. No one in the group showed any frustration, and the points made were very significant. The bishops were unaware of the power they held within the room.

Many believed the meeting had been successful. A conclusion had been reached, and they thought all had been involved. Both the very able chair and the people who had not spoken believed the conclusions reached had been participatory. As they went further in the journey, they began to see one another in a very different way.

The gospels spend a great deal of time looking at the way that God challenged established structures of power through the life of his son Jesus. If taken seriously they challenge completely the way we live as community. If we take them seriously, it will change the way we run our meetings.

Redefining power

Those who followed Jesus shared an understanding of power and glory that runs through most cultures. The disciples wanted their moment in the spotlight; they wanted to be celebrities and to have the benefits of being at the top of the pile. One day James and John approached Jesus to ask him for something. They wanted him to use his power to promote them to be the top disciples and to sit at his right and his left; they wanted to be in the place of honor and glory.

The other ten disciples were furious with James and John for seeking to upstage them, but Jesus challenged them. They were not being offered the chance to be lords ruling over others like tyrants. Rather, they were being shown that to be great was to be a servant of the others. He went even further; the person who wished to be first had to be the slave of all.

Sometimes Bible translators use the word "servant" in this context to make it more palatable, but the Greek word that the New Testament writers use here is *doulos*, and it does mean slave. The practice of slavery in Jesus' time seems somewhat less cruel or dehumanizing compared with most of human history—but it was still slavery. Some were slaves because they were born to slave parents; others were prisoners of war, and some even sold themselves as slaves because they could have a higher standard of life as a slave than if they had to keep struggling to find housing or food on their own. Servants were hired to do particular jobs; slaves were owned by masters or households. Some slaves performed menial household tasks such as foot-washing; others acted as stewards and had a supervisory role or managed the master's finances. Some were well-educated and served as teachers of their master's children. There were social hierarchies among slaves as well as among slave-owners. Slaves of rich masters had all kinds of opportunities that they would never have had on their own. But slaves had no freedom, and their owners could do with them whatever they wanted, including abusing or selling them to someone else. Jesus was fully aware of this when he responded to James' and John's request for power:

> Jesus called them and said to them, "You know that among the Gentiles those whom they recognize as their rulers lord it over them, and their great ones are tyrants over them. But it is not so among you; but whoever wishes to become great among you must be your servant, and whoever wishes to be first among you must be slave of all." (Mark 10:42–44)

When Jesus tells his disciples they are to be slaves of all, he is challenging the freedom they have enjoyed in his company. He uses extreme words so that they cannot miss his point. If Peter had been a slave, he could not have left his boat and family and followed Jesus. Freedom means the power to make choices, but power must not be used to put oneself above others or to support hierarchies. Jesus also had a more radical vision in mind. One act above all others demonstrated the change in power that Jesus envisaged: he washed his disciples' feet.

Foot-washing

In this story of foot-washing, it is our friend Peter who struggles most to understand what is going on. We read in John 13 that Peter is offended and embarrassed by his teacher taking on a role that he himself would not stoop to do.

Washing feet before a meal was an important part of table manners in first-century Jerusalem. Despite Leonardo da

Vinci's painting of the Last Supper, Jesus and his disciples did not sit at chairs around a dining table. The gospels describe Jesus reclining to eat with his friends, which was both the Roman and Jewish practice of the day. They lay on their left side on cushions around a low central table. Given that Jerusalem was a dusty place and sandals were by far the most common form of footwear, it was necessary to wash one's feet before lying closely together on cushions with them on display!

In this meal, Jesus is the host and the disciples the guests. Usually a Gentile slave would have washed all the guests' feet, as it was a lowly task. Since the group was on its own, the guests would have washed their own feet—it would not have occurred to the disciples to wash one another's feet. So when Jesus removes his outer garment, wraps a towel around his waist and kneels down to wash his friends' feet, he is performing a task seen as beneath him; a direct challenge to his disciples. This is Living Reconciliation. Jesus was redefining the power structures of his society in a very threatening manner. It was this story that would inspire another Uganda Archbishop, Silvanus Wani.

Bishops are people of significant power and standing in Africa. The missionary bishops who established the church across Africa over a hundred years ago were part of a colonial movement that assumed order and structure were essential to the establishment of the church. The Tanzanian theologian Mkunga Mtingele has demonstrated how the diocesan structures of Anglicanism replicated the colonial order. Bishops were the equivalent of regional commissioners, ordering their clergy in a structured hierarchy. Archbishops are even more powerful and worthy of great respect.

In 1985 Silvanus Wani, the recently retired Archbishop of Uganda, took a team to lead a day aimed at establishing reconciliation in Koboko, a town far in the north of Uganda. It was his hometown, and the respect shown to him there went even further than in the rest of Uganda. He was the big man coming home. The people, his people, had suffered death and persecution following the war to remove Idi Amin. Amin himself was from Koboko, and the people had been blamed for his rule and exiled to Congo and Sudan. Archbishop Wani was encouraging them to come home, and at the same time was challenging them to live a different way.

Having traveled since early morning, the Archbishop arrived in Koboko from Arua with a team of ten, and was received into a room for tea and cake. In Africa, to drink and eat is not a small matter. Even a cup of tea requires a prayer of thanks and a request for blessing. Since all food is eaten by hand, it is necessary to wash. Hand-washing is more than just hygiene; it is a ritual. The act of hand-washing is an act of service. The water may have come from far away so it is highly valued. In Uganda, the servant washing the hands kneels before the person being served. It is an act of giving and establishes the order of power.

To the amazement of all present, the Archbishop challenged the way things were done. As the special guest, he was approached first by the young woman who had been given the honor of service. When she knelt down, he asked her name. Calling her by name he asked her to stand and, standing himself, took the bowl and towel and seated her in his place. Her hands went up to her face in an attempt to hide her shame. She knew this was against the order of the way things were done and she could be punished for showing such dishonor. He waited patiently for the young woman who eventually offered her hands to be washed. He then continued to wash the hands of those around the room.

The chaplain who had accompanied the archbishop rushed to take the bowl from him, but the archbishop refused. The act of service was his. The chaplain would have opportunities in the future to serve, but now was his time. The message was made clear: if reconciliation was to be lived, it was not just about forgiveness of those who had brought violence; it was about living in a different way, reordering the power structures. Power had been reversed. Amin had been in power and had ruled by violence. He had been overthrown and revenge had been taken. If the vicious circle was to be broken, then the assumed rights and dignities of power needed to be redefined.

Uncomfortable challenge

Just like the young woman in Uganda, when Jesus comes to wash Peter's feet, he blusters and refuses. At first glance it seems as if Peter doesn't understand what is going on, but his reaction demonstrates that he has grasped more of the meaning of Jesus' actions than his fellow disciples. The other disciples seem willing to let Jesus continue, but Peter understands that Jesus is challenging the established order. There is a stand-off, and Jesus makes it clear that unless Peter allows him to wash his feet, he is out of the community.

Peter rallies and asks Jesus to wash also his hands and head, all of his exposed skin, mistaking Jesus' rebuke to be about cleanliness. Jesus' response, however, is much more challenging than the disciple expects:

> After he had washed their feet, had put on his robe, and had returned to the table, he said to them, "Do you know what I have done to you? You call me Teacher and Lord—and you are right, for that is what I am. So if I, your Lord and Teacher, have washed your feet, you also ought to wash one another's feet. For I have set you an example, that you also should do as I have done to you. Very truly, I tell you, servants are not greater than their master, nor are messengers greater than the one who sent them. If you know these things, you are blessed if you do them." (John 13:12–17)

Through the incident over who would sit on Jesus' right and left, and after washing their feet, Jesus tells his disciples how—as his followers—they should behave in terms of power and leadership. Jesus is challenging his disciples not only to not "lord it over" one another but also to live in a way where all are beholden to one another.

Jesus, like Archbishop Wani after him, was breaking the circles and structures of power—and calling his followers to do likewise. This isn't just about inverting power. It isn't about the powerful or those holding authority changing places with those of low status—that is, just using power in a different although more benign way. Jesus' call to be "slaves of all" is not that we merely wash one another's feet, but that we break down the barriers of power that stop us from seeing one another as God sees us. It is not about a group of individuals looking after one another; it is about a sense of belonging to one another in community. This means working together on understanding that all are of equal value in God's eyes because of our diversity, not despite it. Belonging to one another also means realizing that all need to live a different way so that all are included.

Including children

A dispute arose in a church over the style of worship for the all-age service. Some people wanted to use new songs that energized them in their spiritual life and saw the "family service" as an opportunity to bring in new music. Others wanted to root the service in established hymns that maintained a depth of spirituality and connected the children to the past; they wanted to preserve the music they loved for the future of the church. The arguments over worship style were carried on between those who led worship and those within the vestry or church council. Only adults were involved. They spoke on behalf of the children, but used them as an excuse to make their own points and raise their own issues. The actual conflict was about the adults' own different approaches to worship. The resulting compromises to placate the two sides resulted in services that pleased no one, least of all the children.

When someone pointed out that Jesus had placed a child at the center, saying "Whoever welcomes one such child in my name welcomes me..." (Mark 9:36–37), a different approach was considered. The children who regularly came to worship were included in the design of a service. They participated in the choosing of music and, from there, were asked to construct prayers. Soon they were being asked on a regular basis to think in advance about the Bible readings for the coming service. The adult worship leaders took their ideas seriously and included them, often working with them on content. The children took an active part in the direction of the worship, along with a range of adults of all ages. Previously every service had involved a craft activity, which pleased some of the children, but others wanted different components such as games or participatory drama. Placing the children at the heart of the service revolutionized the participation of all and changed the power dynamics.

The children became enthusiastic about the worship they had helped design. They shared ownership with adults and enjoyed the choir as well as the guitar-led action songs. They were respected as people. Some wanted to be up front, and others preferred to stay with their parents; they could be extroverts or introverts and participate in different ways. Inclusion became natural for the design of the service and for the worshiping community.

Including all

There is an extent to which children need guidance and cannot take full responsibility. They need nurture and protection. But they also need to be included. The church also fails and treats adults as children when the adults are excluded from decision-making, whether because of their gender, ethnicity, sexuality, or age (because they are considered too old as well as too young). Decisions are made for people as to where they may be "allowed" to speak or to be heard by advocates speaking on their behalf. This is a contradiction of the way Jesus related to his own community, which should be a challenge to the way we construct ours.

Each Continuing Indaba journey ended with a three-day facilitated conversation. These began with the negotiation of shared "ground rules." Invariably a rule was voiced that people should speak for themselves, not for a group they believed they were representing. For some people this was really hard. They wanted to speak on behalf of women, or "the poor." Others wanted to speak on behalf of those who shared a theological position. The radical change happened when they discovered that they were valued for who they were and did not need to construct a lobby group. Every person was there to be taken seriously, whether they were lay or ordained, young or old, whether they were powerful in their own context or frequently overlooked.

For some this equality was threatening. One bishop spoke up at a meeting, saying that if the women were listened to, he did not want them given the power to tell men what to do. The voices came back saying that this was not the point. It was for all to be heard and valued.

Living Reconciliation also fails if those who were oppressed become oppressors. The walls of separation need to be broken down so that perceptions and structures can be transformed.

However, Living Reconciliation does not end conflict. When face to face and person to person with people who are your companions, it can bring conflict to the surface and make it real. The adults who were arguing over the worship for children still had their issues to face, even after involving the children. For that reason, Living Reconciliation means not only challenging power but also engaging in conflict in a way that is healthy.

* * *

Prayer

> Loving God, who in Jesus showed us power marked by humility and service, sustain and uphold us in and through your strength as we walk the difficult path of following Jesus' example. *Amen.*

Questions to think about

1. What are the power structures you encounter in your daily life?

2. How do you challenge power in your own life, and how is your power challenged?

3. Whose voices are not being heard in your church?

Further thinking

For additional material on the topics discussed in this chapter—including videos, study guides, and further reading—please visit www.living-reconciliation.org.

Chapter 5

Transforming conflict

Conflict is a normal healthy part of human behavior, so we should not be surprised to see it in our church. Even a brief reading of the New Testament shows us that there was considerable friction as the gospel spread and church communities grew. It is how we handle these conflicts that can either strengthen or destroy people and communities. A conflict handled poorly can be open and bitter, poisoning the air for everyone. There is a huge temptation to avoid conflict at all costs. In the long term, this is never healthy or helpful. Some churches may remove people who disagree from positions of leadership. Some people or a group may step away and join a different church, or even found their own church. More frequently, members and leaders just keep their views and their lives to themselves. There is no hope of reconciliation in such action. If we are to Live Reconciliation, then differences need to be faced and conflict has to be acknowledged and transformed.

Living Reconciliation requires facing up to the reality of conflict in a constructive way. In this chapter we will look at the common thread between conflict transformation in the world and in the Church.

Responses to conflict

Let's return to the story of the playground fight in the first chapter. The pattern of fight, forced separation, judgment, and reconciliation seen in the playground is repeated in communities around the world.

When our televisions report news of an atrocity, we may instinctively respond like the teacher. We want to know who is responsible. We want justice for the weeping families and hope for defenseless children. We want the international community to step in and bring order, and we want the conflict to be settled. There is often a demand for a peacekeeping military force to bring about this order. We then seek to punish the guilty. For this, international courts have been set up for calling the culprits to account. We may also reward those who behave well with grants for aid and development. However, the only hope for real and lasting peace comes in the form of reconciliation through conflict transformation.

The problem is that the conflicts that erupt are rarely simple events. The act of stepping in often is to support one side over another. When it comes to attributing guilt, it may not be at all clear where blame is to be placed. It is rarely possible to describe any significant event by one uncontested account, as there are always different perspectives and different histories.

Every side in any conflict sees the same events from their own perspective. These events become part of the cultural context and shape how they see the "other side." Just as in the playground, factions and divisions are perpetuated by a resolution that merely stops the violence at the present moment. The complexity of securing a ceasefire and protecting the innocent can become so overwhelming that the next stage of reconciliation seems impossible.

Despite these difficulties, there are inspiring examples of conflict being transformed. The great figure of Nelson Mandela shines as a beacon for a way of honesty and forgiveness. The process of transforming conflict begins when all are able to come together and realize that differing histories and perspectives need to be faced by those who would seek to extend the war or struggle. This is true for a playground fight or ethnic rivalries with histories that stretch back hundreds of years.

If conflict is not transformed, but merely resolved, small incidents can spark the memories of unforgiven atrocities committed by all sides over a long period of time. Complex mixes of competing grievances are quickly reawakened and there is a return to violence.

History tells us that reconciliation is possible. It is a reality for many—despite the distorted picture of the world we may see on the news.

Stories that emerge from Africa often seem to reflect a stereotype of continual violence that does not represent the truth for millions of people who live in peace and security. These stories can produce a sense of helplessness and the idea that security for a specific group will only come by the elimination of another. In some cases, there are many reasons why this pattern is repeated. But it can be changed.

When the Continuing Indaba project gathered a group of theologians from around Kenya for a consultation in 2009, many of the papers and reflections were deeply significant; but one stood out as potentially life-changing. John Mark Oduor—a worship leader at All Saints Cathedral in Nairobi—reflected:

> The drumbeat of terror, fear, conflict, tension and shedding of blood has become such a part of the African life over the last few decades that it is almost hard to imagine that there can be any other way to be *Africa*. The prevailing drumbeat of conflict was so loud in our ears that no other beat could be heard.[1]

He called for a new drum proclaiming a completely different beat.

Odour identified that in the face of horrific violence and deep-rooted injustice the common responses were "only managed temporary solutions, treating symptoms and signs but not the real disease."[2] People still danced to the same drums that still beat the same rhythms. Unless the drum itself was changed, the old ways would be repeated.

In his paper, Odour set out to identify some of the drums that drew people into conflict. The first was the drum of silence. Some people just close their eyes and hope that conflict would go away. They remain silent in the face of injustice. This silent drum does not face up to the causes of conflict and nothing changes. It is the drum of fear. People remain silent out of fear.

The loud drumbeat is that of blame. This beat blasts out political rhetoric. Oduor says: "Everyone seems to know who was responsible and who should be penalized and who should be arrested and imprisoned but nobody does a thing or owns up and admits, 'I'm responsible.'"[3] This drum is sounded by people who would not themselves fight, but they create cultures of fear and resentment. They whip up a "fighting spirit" in those they send into battle. All sides talk of conspiracies by others to destroy them. Any offers of peace are rejected as having hidden agendas.

The drum of blame calls for outside judgment; it asks for intervention from the international community to take responsibility and provide external justice. This places the responsibility on someone else and avoids the hard task of facing up to the root causes.

The drumbeat of blame then turns to call for intervention from God. Oduor noticed how the prayers of many Kenyans called on God to destroy their enemies:

> Many curse and hope their curses will have generational effect. They curse the perpetrators and wish their children and families will live to regret all their days or may be doomed in the land they or their parents grabbed, stole or acquired through dubious and illegal means. They call on God to "fix" their enemies. They conveniently quote the psalmist, "let God arise and his enemies be scattered...Let them run in seven different directions." (Psalm 68.1)[4]

This response of turning to God to intervene and destroy our enemies is not limited to Africa; it has been a feature of wars across the world for generations. Such sentiments are summed up in the famous call to arms of Shakespeare's *Henry V* as he calls his men: "Once more unto the breach, dear friends, once more."[5] He reminds the soldiers not to dishonor their mothers and concludes with the battle cry that invokes God to intervene on their side and their side alone. The similarities between this speech and Oduor's analysis are striking.

However, Oduor goes on to show how in reality the drum of blame leads to despair. Silence in the face of injustice encourages the powerful to continue in their ways. Blame enables all sides to cast themselves as victims. The international community is

rarely effective and often unable to offer clear judgm
does not intervene to destroy those who have been 1
enemies. There is no quick fix to any long-term co
these drums are false in the hope they offer.

In response, Oduor proposed the building of a new drum to sound out a new drumbeat, a drum that calls us all to a place of meeting—an *Indaba* or, in the language of Kenya, a *Baraza*.

The new drum

The sound emerging from an African drum is determined by the wooden tree trunk that forms the body of the drum. The trunk is "the defining material that gives the drum the shape, size, and ultimately its unique type of sound."[5] Oduor identified that if the new drum is to beat out the call of unconditional love, Jesus had to be the core.

The type of sound in an African drum is determined by the skin. Oduor wanted to avoid the hippo skin of revenge for "the genuine leather of love, forgiveness and grace."[6] He identified the mission of reconciliation as the skin for the drum.

What is really interesting about Oduor's drum is not just the trunk and the skin but how they are held together. In an African drum, the key elements in producing a sound are the strings that keep the skin tight. These strings are essential in ensuring that the drum produces its sound. In identifying five "strings," Oduor explored how we are to Live Reconciliation.

...ıe first string on the drum is *relationship*. There is a need to see one another as part of a community that stands together in all circumstances. "A prerequisite to understanding the community and dealing with its issues was in being part of the community, to be in relationship."[7]

Once community is established, *conversation* is possible. Oduor says that within his Luo culture, "the community appreciated the diversity within itself. They expected people to hold different opinions but everyone was allowed to talk and share their ideas. There was room for everyone."[9] Jesus also spoke of conflict transformation in this way, encouraging face-to-face conversation in the context of conflict (Matthew 18).

The third string is *a place of meeting*—a fellowship, an Indaba, or Baraza. In the Luo culture a tree of meeting was set aside as a place where the community could come to discuss concerns and share one another's "burdens, weaknesses, strengths, and encouragements."[10]

As the community comes together, there must be an increasing *appreciation of our uniqueness*. This is the fourth string, and it allows members to use their best qualities, skills, talents to enrich the life of the community. The interplay between individual uniqueness community wholeness is understood in African societies. Oduor writes: "Among the Luo, one's identity was not based on individual name or individuality as such, but tied to the identity of the whole community."[11]

The final string is the hardest part of community life. It is *forgiveness and belonging*. Oduor quotes Richard Gehman who says, "Forgiveness is costly and difficult. True forgiveness is the hardest thing in the universe, our idea of justice pulls the other way."[12] It means living out and not just reciting the Lord's Prayer, and forgiving others as we are forgiven ourselves. Oduor again remembers the traditions of his people when he says:

> The Luo called forgiveness *wena*, which literally translated means, "Leave me" or "let me go." It gave the victim the prerogative or the final say after or during forgiveness has taken place. After forgiveness the community encouraged that victim and the aggressor to "walk together," as a demonstration of "belonging together."[13]

The five strings of relationship, conversation, a place of meeting, appreciation of our uniqueness, and forgiving and belonging are the way in which the new drum beats out the rhythm of unconditional love and reconciliation. This new drumbeat is needed in our church and in our world.

Conflict in the Christian community

National and international news agencies not only often portray a distorted view of Africa, they also give a distorted view of conflict within the church. Lively, growing churches

ming the lives of people individually and within
nmunities are rarely reported upon. Divisions and
...ents, on the other hand, get media attention because
they are "news." The Church, however, has been a place of
division from the beginning. If we are to Live Reconciliation
in our world, we need to live it in our churches. The letters
of Paul focus on the conflicts emerging in the early Christian
community, and they offer us insight into the ways of
reconciliation. But in order for us to understand them, we
need to consider how they arose.

The first churches that emerged after the day of Pentecost
were bursting with energy and enthusiasm. Peter and his
friends were able to speak with power, to resist persecution,
and saw miracles in response to their prayers. The growth
in numbers was extraordinary and those who were baptized
dedicated their lives by sharing their possessions. They were
a community. The early days did not last long, and there was
one issue above all others that caused a split. This issue was the
inclusion of Gentiles.

The initial outpouring of the Holy Spirit was upon Jews from
across the known world. The ravages of war through centuries
meant that Jewish people not only were living in communities
in the towns and cities of the Roman Empire, but also in great
numbers in the Persian Empire to the east and in Ethiopia to
the south. When Jesus told Peter and the others that they were
to take his message to the ends of the world, they assumed it
was to these Jewish communities far away. The Holy Spirit had
other ideas.

In Acts 10 we read about Cornelius, a centurion of the Italian legion based in a town built to enforce occupation by Herod and named in honor of Augustus Caesar. Cornelius, a man of prayer who served the poor, was at home in Caesarea when an angel appeared telling him to call Peter to visit him. After consulting with friends, he decided to do as he was asked and sent out people to bring Peter to him.

Peter was staying at Joppa—about thirty miles away. He was elated by the growth of the church and the miracles he had witnessed. He also was tired. He took time to pray but was distracted by hunger; when he fell asleep, thoughts of food filled his dream. Instead of a kosher banquet, he was faced by the image of all kinds of animals that were forbidden to be eaten under Jewish law. Within the dream he heard the words, "Get up Peter. Kill and eat." Peter recoiled, protesting his purity. Three times the voice challenged him with the words, "Do not call anything impure that God has made clean."

When the messengers arrived from Cornelius, he invited them in as guests. In the text of Acts 10 this is a simple line. However, it was not a simple act. Peter welcomed Gentiles as guests. He presumably ate with them and crossed the barriers of separation. He then traveled with them, but he did not travel alone. He was accompanied by other Jews who also would have had questions about the rightness of what they were doing.

On entering the home of Cornelius, Peter found a community waiting for him, eager to hear the message he had to bring. As he was preaching, these Gentiles began to speak in tongues and to praise God. Peter and his friends were amazed, and it was then that they realized that the gospel really was for all—for Jew and Gentile. They recognized the Holy Spirit at work in the people, and they formally marked their inclusion into the Christian community through baptism, without demanding that the men be circumcised.

The shock of such an act reverberated through the Christian community, and Peter was called to account. His initial explanation of the events was greeted with joy, but the implications were to cause serious divisions in the church over the coming decades.

The identity of the church began to change, especially when Barnabas and Paul began targeting Gentile audiences (the church at Antioch, for example, as reported in Acts 13:46–48). In Jerusalem the church remained largely Jewish, but in Syria and Cyprus the Gentile mission took hold. This led to the forming of separate parties and to the Jewish Christians making demands on the Gentile converts that Paul considered inappropriate. The question was raised as to whether Gentile converts should be circumcised and should follow the Jewish laws, especially those associated with eating. Conflict emerged and the community was faced with the question of how it could be resolved.

Ending conflict?

The aim for the leaders of the Church was to end the conflict. The method they used was to bring the issues to a council of elders. Such processes are often seen as the best way to ensure an even-handed decision. If groups have significant disagreement and have reached an impasse, it is logically assumed that a council of disinterested people who are respected by all can formulate a judgment and end the conflict.

Paul and Barnabas were called before a council of elders headed by James (see Acts 15). On their side was Peter. They were opposed by faithful Christians who feared the loss of identity if Gentiles were not expected to become Jews. The evidence was studied, testimonies were heard, scriptures were consulted, and James gave his judgment. On the whole, it favored Paul, in that circumcision was not required of the Gentile converts. On the other hand it did reinforce the food purity laws as a requirement, pleasing the other group. The judgment could be seen as a middle way—an even-handed judgment. Neither side was entirely satisfied with the middle-way judgment, but it could end the conflict so that all could get back to mission.

For the two groups, the judgment appeared to have made little difference. Paul left the interpretation of the rules to the Gentile Christians he was serving. The only demand he made was that they offer financial aid to the Jewish Christians of Jerusalem (Galatians 2:10). The "circumcision group" grew in strength in their heartlands and sent out their people to the churches that Paul had founded, spreading disunity to churches as far away as Philippi in modern-day northern Greece.

As time went on, Paul founded more and more churches and kept in contact with them, both through messengers traveling in person and through letters. As we read some of these letters that survive in the New Testament, we can see Paul's increasing anger over the actions of the circumcision party. In Philippians he berates them as "dogs" and "evildoers" who mutilated the flesh. He tells the Colossians not to listen to the circumcision party and berates the Galatians for their foolishness in abandoning the way of faith.

The conflict had not been solved and was spreading. The issue was over a shared meal table. Paul told the Galatians that even Peter was recruited to the side of those who insisted on law over grace, by refusing to eat with Gentile Christians in Ephesus. Peter might know that the Gentiles were in receipt of the Holy Spirit, but he followed his Jewish Christian friends in refusing to eat with them and so denied that they were part of the same family. In response, Paul confronted Peter face to face. He called on him to remember his own story and to remember that no one was saved by living the law.

When the Church through the ages has faced deep and complex divisions, there is always the temptation to replicate the Jerusalem Council. However, Paul's account of his experience in Galatians does not indicate any sense that he felt constrained by its ruling. He makes it quite clear that he is not a servant of people—however elevated they might be—his loyalty is to Christ. When, in his letters, he calls on communities to stand firm in the faith, he does not appeal to councils or any earthly higher authority. Again and again he implores his friends to remember the core message of the gospel, that Jesus had destroyed the law of sin and death and was Love. His appeal was to the individuals themselves to remember why they had committed their life to Christ, not to the statement of some authoritative group of elders.

Paul may have felt tempted to use such methods himself when he was confronted by a different kind of division in the church in Corinth. The problem in Corinth was that the Christians were separating into ever increasing numbers of house churches, each seeking its own way. Paul did not pass judgment on who was right or wrong nor did he set up a council to pass judgment. If you read 1 Corinthians as a whole, it is impossible to know what they were really arguing about. Instead of focusing on solutions to arguments, Paul asks them to remember that Christ died and rose again, and that the most excellent way is love. He calls them to return from their flight into disparate groups and to reconcile in Christ. In the end there is only one Church, understood and experienced in diversity.

Paul called the Corinthian church, particularly in chapters 11 and 12 of 1 Corinthians, to re-establish their relationship, to engage in conversation, come to a shared place of mee the eucharist, to appreciate the uniqueness of each of the body, and to forgive and belong. He called for the five strings of John Mark Oduor's drum to be pulled tight to sound out reconciliation in the Church and the world.

The Ephesian moment

Toward the end of Paul's life there began to be a change in the location of power in the Church. The Gentile church was growing, and the Jewish core was becoming isolated. The letter to the Ephesians marks the point at which the competing struggle is met by both opportunity and danger. This moment in time was identified by Andrew Walls in an essay published in 2002, called "The Ephesian Moment."[14]

Walls argued that the defining marker of division between Jew and Gentile was the meal table. Jews ate only with Jews. Since the defining act of Christian worship was a meal, the only possible result was the emergence of two parallel communities in one place. In response, the letter to the Ephesians sets out a different vision with only *one* Christian community.

In Ephesians 2:11–22, it is made clear that the Gentiles are included among the people of God, along with the Jewish people. The writer tells the Gentiles, "you are no longer strangers and aliens, but you are citizens with the saints and also members of the household of God" (Ephesians 2:19). In his analysis of this passage, Walls argues that if Christ is the ʳd of the whole world, "the church must be diverse because ʟ ʟⁱᵗy is diverse; it must be one because Christ is one."[15]

The believers, both Jewish and Gentile, are to be built together spiritually into a new temple, a dwelling place for God.

The familiar motif of the Body of Christ is used in a specific manner in Ephesians 4. Its use in 1 Corinthians is about the differing ministries and callings of the people. In Ephesians this is echoed, but the focus is on the unification of diverse people into a living organic unit. In Ephesians 4:1–6, Paul claims that in order to do this they need to display humility, gentleness, and patience. They are to bear with one another in love so they can maintain the unity of the body in their diversity. They are many, but there is only one body because there is only "one Lord, one faith, one baptism, one God." It is absolutely clear that such unity is not easy, and it requires "speaking the truth in love"—but it is the consequence of the saving act of Christ in the world. There cannot be two churches in one place divided by cultural differences; there is only one Church. According to Walls, "the very height of Christ's full stature is reached only by the coming together of the different cultural entities into the body of Christ. Only 'together,' not on our own, can we reach his full stature."[16]

The Ephesian moment came and went. The staggering growth of the Gentile church was matched by the increasing persecution of all Jewish people and the establishment of a church that, at its best, respected diversity among its Gentile adherents but frequently acted as an agent of anti-Semitism, and the vision was lost. At worst, Christianity became completely linked to specific cultures, and what arose were numerous mono-cultural expressions of Christianity, each believing they were the only true expression of faith in God.

Today we have new opportunities. The church is growing throughout the world, and face-to-face contact with Christians from a multitude of cultures is possible for all of us. But we are confronted by two dangers. The first is the drive to establish our version of Christianity as the correct version and to force conformity on others. The second is to decide that all are equally valid and authentic so long as they are kept in isolation. Both ways are a denial of the way of Christ.

The way of Living Reconciliation is the difficult process of being "built together spiritually" across differences that were unimaginable to Paul as he considered the ends of the earth. We require humility to know that we do not hold the whole truth. We require patience to stick with people who are living in a manner that at times is deeply shocking to us. We need the courage to speak the truth in love and to risk being misunderstood or even rejected.

Living Reconciliation in the Anglican Communion

Throughout the 1980s, it was assumed by many people that the Anglican Communion would split over the ordination of women, first as priests and then as bishops. People sought conclusive answers from the Lambeth Conference and then from commissions set up to preserve the greatest degree of unity in a divided communion. The proponents and opponents of women's ordination established themselves in groups and perfected their arguments, rejoicing at victories, and reorganizing at any setback. Lobby groups formed on both sides. As these groups thrived, systems were invented to maintain order—but relationships suffered.

In some churches, women's ordination was an orderly process; in others it was surrounded by great strife. In some situations, boundaries were transgressed in a felt commitment to a practical need or to justice. In other contexts, boundaries were defined and people settled into them. Too often a truce or peace was declared without reconciliation. Some churches within the Anglican Communion continue to not ordain women.

In 2010 the bishops of Saldanha Bay in South Africa, Ho in Ghana, and Mbeere in Kenya agreed on a partnership among their dioceses and embarked on a Continuing Indaba journey. They laughed and prayed together and signed an agreement of partnership. They knew the journey would not be easy, but they could not know how difficult the common journey would be.

When their teams of eight people gathered for their first encounter together in South Africa, they began to form relationships. They discovered both strong resonances and deep differences, not only among their African cultures but also in their Anglicanism. These differences were clearly seen in the different responses to the ordination of women as priests.

The Diocese of Ho is a traditional Anglo-Catholic diocese, in which women have an active role in ministry but are not ordained. The Diocese of Mbeere is an evangelical diocese influenced by the East African Revival, which sees women's ordination as biblical and has many ordained women. Saldanha Bay is a modern catholic diocese shaped by the history of South Africa where women's ordination is a vital expression of equality and justice. The Kenyan and South African dioceses were passionately in favor of the ordination of women. However, their reasoning and reference points were very different. This meant that the dynamics were not simply two against one; there was a three-way engagement. Through their journey together, there were moments of intense conflict between the members of the teams. There were times when walking away and not finishing the journey together was a real option.

There were two women priests in the group, both from Kenya, and during the teams' first meeting together in South Africa there was a lively engagement on the topic of ordination. However, when they traveled to Ghana, the differences came to the fore when part of the group felt that these two members were being excluded because they were ordained women. The topic of women's ordination and their differing views had moved from being a background note to becoming personal— not just to the two ordained women but to the whole group. The tensions escalated, and the three separate teams began to wonder if there was any benefit in their relationship. They seriously contemplated returning home to live without the others. In making the decision to continue on their journey together without resolving the conflict, without coming to one mind, they chose the much harder path. It was not an easy decision to make; it required sacrificing ideas of a tidy outcome and of living in a "perfect" church.

The last of their three journeys together was to Mbeere, Kenya. Toward the end of their time, the group took part in a community reconciliation event at a place called Nyaangwa. Bishop Moses had been using Indaba principles to resolve a dispute that had been tearing apart the local community, setting neighbor against neighbor for over sixty years. The elders of the clans in dispute had met together and agreed that the time for reconciliation had come. In the words of John Mark Oduor, they had decided to change the drumbeat. To do so, it was necessary to call the whole community together, for them to dance to the new drumbeat, and transform the conflict so that they could Live Reconciliation.

It was important to the local community that there were external witnesses to their reconciliation. The group from Saldanha Bay, Ho, and the wider Diocese of Mbeere were called to gather with them. Together they took part in a liturgical event of reconciliation and healing. Through their active participation in community celebration, they bore witness to the transformation of the historical conflict.

Witnessing this moment of transformation in the life of the community at Nyaangwa was transformational for the Indaba group too. Being called to bear witness to this act of reconciliation brought new energy to their journey together. It was on their mind when they came together to discuss their journey. Their thoughts and feelings around the different views on women's ordination were still high on their agenda. For some, the need to persuade others was still strong and led to anger and confrontation. But primarily there were relationships. In going beyond what it meant to change the persons who you know are wrong, and journeying alongside them, they discovered reconciliation. Today their journey of partnership continues. They have discovered that they do not need to agree on everything to pray with and support one another.

Dancing to a new drumbeat

The old drum has beaten to the tune of an instant fix. It called out with urgency to solve a problem now. Our world is ever faster and any solution that is not instant often is regarded as insufficient. Ephesians talks of the need for patience, the importance of bearing with one another in love, and of growing into a holy temple. These are slow words that emphasize relationships and not quick-fix words that emphasize solutions. The old drum calls out the sound of divide, decide, and "do as I say." The new drum beats out the call to build relationships, to recognize uniqueness, to converse in a place of meeting, and to know we belong to one another as we live out the prayer of Jesus in forgiving one another as we are forgiven.

The old drumbeat is one of impatience for perfection. Justice must be administered now. Truth must be established immediately. The drumbeat of Living Reconciliation is one that lives in a world of complexity. We are on a journey to truth and justice. Living Reconciliation means we are always hungry for more truth and more justice.

The conflicts in your parish are not solved in isolation. It is only when you Live Reconciliation in the world that you can Live Reconciliation in the Church. Living Reconciliation in the world is impossible if you are not prepared to walk the same way in your own Christian community. This involves taking time. There can be huge pressures to make decisions, and people are often asked to put aside divisions in order to make decisions. However, good decisions are rarely possible unless there is a sense of common understanding.

Taking time to dance to the new drumbeat can make seemingly impossible decisions seem far easier, as all are committing to a common direction. In the end the process can be quicker than if a "quick" decision had been lost in a remerging, unresolved conflict. It can seem much safer to make decisions that do not open up conflict. However. it is only through having the courage to take risks together that conflict can be transformed.

* * *

Prayer

> Loving God, who set the drumbeat of love at creation, guide our feet in the rhythm of your footsteps, that we might live the complex dance of reconciliation together. *Amen.*

Questions to think about

1. What are the negative drumbeats in your church and community?

2. How could you hear that drumbeat differently? Does the drumbeat need to change?

3. What positive drumbeats do your church and community need? How can you be part of that change?

Further thinking

For additional material on the topics discussed in this chapter—including videos, study guides, and further reading—please visit www.living-reconciliation.org.

Chapter 6

Risk

Throughout the scriptures, there is a tension between the perfection we hope for and the reality we live in. This is the "now and not yet" of the experience of the kingdom. Jesus announces that the kingdom is near, but it is also far away. It is both with us in our life in Christ and ahead of us as we wait for his return. In the Eucharist we affirm this as we declare:

> Christ has died:
> Christ is risen:
> Christ will come again.

To Live Reconciliation is to take seriously the reality of living in anticipation of the coming kingdom. We are on a journey of hope toward a state where, as in 1 Corinthians 13:10–13, things will be complete: a place where we will know God, just as God knows us, and where there will be justice and peace. On that journey we have to live in a real world, where we are journeying toward truth and struggling for justice.

This chapter is aimed at taking you further into the task of Living Reconciliation. It seeks to go beyond the desire for quick solutions and show how important it is to have the patience talked about in Ephesians. To do this we need to risk a return when we run away, avoid the desire for someone else to decide a matter, and let go of the need for hasty solutions.

Flight and return

Abraham and Sarah had a problem. God had promised Abraham that he would make him the father of a mighty nation, but they had no children, and they were both getting older and older. Sarah suggested a quick fix to the problem. Abraham could sleep with her Egyptian slave girl Hagar, and they could then adopt the child. However, when Hagar conceived, she began to belittle Sarah, humiliating her in her inability to bear a child. Jealousy provoked anger in Sarah, and she sought another quick solution by telling Abraham to solve the problem. Ignoring his own role in the situation, he chose the drumbeat of silence, refusing to play any part in their conflict and telling Sarah to do whatever she wanted. When Sarah took out her anger on Hagar, the slave girl fled. Running away from the conflict seemed to be the best, perhaps the only, solution.

In this biblical story the desire for instant solutions compounded the problem until separation was seen as the only option. Emily Onyango, a Kenyan theologian, grappled with this text following her own flight from conflict in 2007. She argues that flight is important if it gives time for reflection, but it is only helpful if it is followed by return.

Onyango points out that, in fleeing, Hagar is found by the angel of the Lord, God in visible form, who addresses her by name. By using her name he affirms that she is human. In asking her where she has come from and where she is going, Hagar is forced to reflect on the reality of her situation.

> Flight, therefore, becomes an opportunity to meet God, listen to God and to obey the instructions of God. Listening to God becomes a spring board for self-reflection and also to return. God corrects Hagar but also affirms her and gives her hope.[1]

Hagar is ordered to return. In humility she must take back her role as a slave of Sarah—but also with a hope. She is promised that her descendants will become a great nation, a nation always at war and always in conflict, but great nevertheless.

> Hagar is therefore ordered to go back to her mistress. She is also not innocent and has wronged Sarah, both had wronged each other, and the flight was not helping but alienating them. However, after encountering and listening to God Hagar returned to her mistress.[2]

The shortcuts to solving the issues resulted in a complex entanglement of competing injustices, but they also led to new hopes and new opportunities. In the end it was impossible to neatly resolve the mess created. All had to take responsibility for the part they played. Abraham did this by naming his son and so took responsibility for him. Sarah was never able to accept Hagar and her son, and eventually sent her away. Without forgiveness, there was no future for the relationship.

This personal failure of reconciliation became the source of ongoing conflict that spread to competing tribes and warring nations. The failure to reconcile created a rift that is still referred to by those on opposing sides in Middle East conflicts. Some Muslim Arabs see themselves as descendants of Hagar's son Ishmael, still at war with Sarah's son Isaac. Short-term solutions that fail to engender reconciliation can lead to endless disputes.

For Onyango, flight presented the opportunity to encounter God and to return to reconcile with others. It also enabled her to make sense of the friction within the Anglican Communion. Those who heard her present the Bible study for the first time knew that she was a member of the theological commission of the Global Anglican Futures Conference (GAFCON) that had its first meeting just before the 2008 Lambeth Conference. GAFCON had been attended by Anglicans from around the world, including many who refused to attend the Lambeth Conference. Immediately, she concluded, they tried to identify various players in the Communion disputes with those in the story. They started to argue among themselves if it was the GAFCON bishops or The Episcopal Church bishops who were like Sarah or Abraham. They then turned to her to ask her to identify the sides in the disputes with the biblical characters.

Emily Onyango just smiled. Her point was that we all exhibit the traits of all the characters at some time in our lives. We are all in some ways Hagar, Sarah, and Abraham. We all flee from situations and conflict; we all need to learn to listen to God, take responsibility, and Live Reconciliation.

Rushing to a conclusion

The journey of reconciliation starts from where we are, not from where we think we ought to be. When the four different groups began their Continuing Indaba journeys in the pilot program, most participants wanted to have the difficult conversations right away. There is a huge risk in forming relationships with those whom we know we disagree before setting out our positions and determining who is right. There also is a desire to clear away any potential conflict at the start of a journey.

This is where the Continuing Indaba process differs from other approaches to building partnerships across the Anglican Communion. The aims are not to impose a solution that is negotiated through a consensus process between archbishops and eminent theologians. It aims not to exclude any voice from the table and not to hide from the real and deep differences within Anglicanism. It seeks to set out a pattern for building relationships as a healthy way to transform conflict together. The creation of safe space for honest conversation allows genuine anger to be expressed within the family of Christ.

It is a place where repentance can be present and attitudes can change without the requirement to conform to a single viewpoint. Diversity is still valued and numerous complex relationships are developed in the journey together. It is a place where Christ is at the center.

In reflecting on being part of the Diocese of Toronto team, Bishop Linda Nicholls highlighted the importance of taking time:

> Although our current generation is steeped in communication possibilities it is still challenging to hear and understand those whose context is different from my own. The Continuing Indaba process proved again, to me, the deep importance of both time and place in listening to others. The opportunity to spend time together not only in intense conversation but also around the table for meals, in worship, in travel and in play deepened the bonds of human connection that build trust in the relationships. That time cannot be short-circuited for the sake of efficiency. Building trust is a slow and delicate process of mutual engagement. Living together in the context of the other experientially changed perceptions as the milieu of the culture and place added depth to the conversations. I became more conscious of the impact of history on the development

of the church in a particular place and of both the similarities and differences with our church history in Canada. I am profoundly grateful for the opportunity to engage with my brothers and sisters in Hong Kong and Jamaica and to bring home the importance of "indaba" for strengthening our life in the Church, recognizing that we must be willing to commit the time to live into it and, wherever possible, experience the context of the other more fully.[3]

Coming to know one another, discovering diversity, challenging and being challenged, discovering anew the power dynamics in our own contexts, realizing that we need one another's perspective to see clearly, are all steps along the journey of Living Reconciliation—they are not prerequisites. To avoid conflict and stay at a superficial level of relationship is tempting, but without taking the risk of going deeper we cannot hope to truly transform conflict into energy for flourishing and mission.

Suzanne Lawson, one of the Canadian delegates to the Anglican Consultative Council (ACC), shared her experience as part of the Toronto Indaba team during the 2012 ACC meeting in New Zealand. She spoke to the group of Anglicans gathered from around the globe about the importance of the process of coming to know one another and to build trust before having purposeful and meaningful conversation:

It takes honest effort to build meaningful and lasting relationships...something that shouldn't surprise any of us who have been in committed relationships. Love at first sight doesn't work for longstanding complex relationships with those who don't look like us and don't share the kind of life we have had.

I particularly learned the value of asking questions. I've been very good at asking questions in the past...but the sneaky kind of question that will bring the conversation to my point of view. Not the deep kind of question that actually allows all of us in dialogue to go more deeply into the topic under discussion.[4]

Suzanne described with enthusiasm other things she had learned. These included the importance of having the people being "talked about" be part of the discussion, and the need to throw away stereotypes and encounter individuals instead. She concluded with a rousing challenge to the church from her experience of the relationship among Hong Kong, Toronto, and Jamaica:

What unites us is our commitment to God and to God's mission...we didn't have to agree [in order] to love one another. Few of us changed our minds on anything, but we all ended up with twenty-three new best friends.[5]

These friendships have forever changed the dioceses, parish churches, and provinces involved. People do things differently with the skills and the hope they gained on the Continuing Indaba journey. The new perspectives these global friendships offer on local issues give fresh energy for mission.

Leading reconciliation

Leading a community into reconciliation requires skilled and imaginative leadership. When conflict emerges, leaders come under intense pressure to manage the situation in order to reduce risk. In churches, bishops and parish priests are under immense pressure to hold the center line and produce a result where everyone is happy. Holding the middle way sounds very Anglican, but it also can have the effect of increasing polarization. In response, it is common for lobby groups to emerge, representing both sides in an argument. If they feel belittled or ignored, they seek to raise the stakes. They can be tempted to end the conflict by defeating their opponents. If there is to be reconciliation, there is a need to take the risk of living with diversity and the conflict that requires.

The constant attempt to find a middle way was seen in the debates over female bishops in the Church of England. Over a period of many years, the hierarchy of the Church appointed commissions to satisfy the demands of the majority who wanted women to be bishops and the minority who were seeking legal protections to assure their integrity would be honored. As the decisive votes approached, the voices on both sides began to speak loudly. When the motion before the synod that would have allowed female bishops and provided a limited level of legal protection for opponents failed, there was an initial call to arms. The lobby groups, especially those against the legislation, demanded to be heard.

It was at this point when the bishops of the Church of England took leadership seriously. They called for a different approach. At the following General Synod, they set aside a whole day for members to talk to one another in groups of about twenty-five. Each group was professionally facilitated, helping members to speak directly to one another. As the day progressed, the synod members began to establish trust and hear one another in a new way.

The bishops' leadership challenged the members of the General Synod to find common ground in their understanding, and a way forward. The change was remarkable. In the parliamentary-style debate, members had spoken on behalf of their lobby group as well as themselves to an anonymous crowd. In the close confines of often uncomfortable rooms they spoke for themselves to people whose reactions they could see. Objectified "enemies" started to be known as real people with their own hopes and fears. They spoke to people whom they began to know and understand, and they expected to be heard as individuals within a community as well. In opening up the dialogue, unexpected ways forward were found. They were imperfect and incomplete, but were seen as positive steps forward on a journey together.

In reporting back, members spoke of a profound change. They told of buying drinks at the bar for people they had previously only glowered at. They talked of establishing trust and the need to carry forward this method into the future. They spoke of the significance of the change in the way of doing things, as much as the change in outcome. The process had been risky because when it began the outcome was unpredictable, but taking the risk of trusting the people of God and the Spirit of God working among them had been life-giving.

Truth-telling

Leadership that creates space for all to be heard and to hear takes a great deal of skill and requires deep commitment. It is very risky, as the solutions to conflict are rarely obvious or easy. It means trusting in God and in one another. The following story from the Continuing Indaba journey of the dioceses of El Camino Real, Western Tanganyika, and Gloucester illustrates the pain, difficulty, importance, and joy of speaking the truth in relationships of diversity.

As we learned in chapter 3, the three bishops from California, Gloucester, and Western Tanganyika had formed a close personal bond. They enjoyed being with one another and saw their relationship as transformative. This relationship was consciously built across the divides in the Anglican Communion, which included differing attitudes toward gay and lesbian people. It took a step of faith to extend this journey to the lay and ordained members of their dioceses. One way they took this step was by participating in the Continuing Indaba program.

Early in the journey the teams attempted to speak about the subject of human sexuality in an abstract way, but this had floundered on the use of language. A member of the American team had started to speak of "straight" people and it quickly became clear that there was no Swahili translation for either the word or the concept.

In the West, the words used to describe human sexuality have developed and changed over the years, and are in a constant process of changing. They have moved from words that describe others in pejorative or scientific ways to words that are chosen by individuals and communities themselves. "Straight" is not a simple word to explain; it is understood only in the context of western life.

In Tanzania, where same-sex relationships are illegal, new words have not emerged into common speech, given that people are not safe to own such identities. People in Tanzania are defined by gender, tribe, and religion. They are identified by social standing in the community and whether they have children. There are no words to define someone as heterosexual because there is no obvious alternative; and so there is no word for "straight" in Swahili. All words for anyone who is not heterosexual are pejorative.

The twenty-four people journeying together were chosen because of their skills and commitments. These included their ability to work with young people, their history of transforming communities struggling with poverty, and their skills as theologians. Among them was Rob, an unmarried man and a deacon in the Diocese of El Camino Real, who had given up a comfortable life as a banker to work alongside the poor in California. Rob has an ability to get along with anyone and was immediately popular within the journeying community. He struck up a particular relationship with Gervas from Kasulu in Tanzania.

When the teams met for the second time, in California, Rob was delighted to welcome his friends to his home diocese. As the journey continued, he became increasingly uncomfortable with the reality that Gervas did not know that Rob was gay. For Gervas, being gay and being Christian could not go together. The developing friendship did not automatically create the space for the conversation to happen. If Rob had immediately spoken of this prior to the forming of relationships, others could have rejected him right then. He would have been hurt and angry, but he would have walked away from people he barely knew. The stakes had risen. To come out now was to risk deep friendship and rejection by people he had come to love.

This also created a dilemma for those who were overseeing the process. The relationship among the three dioceses had become very special, and Rob coming out could destroy at a stroke what had been built up over several years. How could the truth emerge in a way that was not hurtful to Rob or to the others who valued his friendship, or to the relationship that these dioceses had built with one another?

The opportunity for truth-telling came in the most unexpected of places and in the most unexpected of ways. One November evening the teams were invited into a Mexican-led church in San Jose. The church, which has embraced the cultures of Hispanic people, exudes vibrancy. It has also become a home to Hawaiian people worshiping in their way, and to a small community of First Nations people.[6] Also known as Indigenous or Native Americans, First Nations people are a tiny minority in this region. They struggle to find a way to live that draws upon their cultural heritage, and they have found a place at St. Philip's to maintain their identity in the midst of a multicultural parish.

After the teams arrived at St. Philip's, they were taken by a First Nation's Episcopal priest to see a sweat lodge, a place of ritual cleansing in his culture. There, they were welcomed by an elder of the community in a ceremony that involved smudging. The elder had gathered herbs, mainly sage, and had lit a fire. As the teams gathered round, he lit the herbs in a bowl and induced smoke that he ritually blew toward each person gathered. He did this as a welcome and to cleanse. He followed this with a spoken welcome and a spiritual song to the creator God.

The unexpected event was both moving and startling. Bishop Mary Gray-Reeves as host apologized for the group's lack of preparation. Her intention was that they would have seen a building and heard about First Nations people. She had not intended to bring the group unprepared into a ceremony. The Tanzanians asked if the ceremony was like the indigenous worship they had been asked to abandon as Satanism by the incoming missionaries. The English team was largely puzzled.

The First Nations men and women had spoken almost exclusively of Father God, not of Jesus, and the next day this led to a group discussion of their history, including the genocide of Indigenous people in the name of Christ. The population figures indicate an 80 percent decline in the numbers of First Nations or Indigenous peoples during the missionary years. Much of that was due to disease introduced unintentionally by the immigrants, but the spread of disease was heightened by their being forced to live in missions controlled by the church. There they were divided into separate compounds for men and women, where contact was limited even between husbands and wives. Much of the population was effectively wiped out in the name of Christ.

As this was explained, a young white member of the Californian team broke down. This was the first time he had been asked to face the real implications of the dominating power that the white incomers had exerted in California over hundreds of years. This power had given him education and opportunity. The same events had marked the lives of Indigenous people by an opposite trajectory. Rob was the perfect person to hear the pain and help it to be used effectively. He had reached out in the same way earlier in the day to a young member who was experiencing the same inequalities of power in her life and the lives of those she loved.

When the group gathered the next day to discuss the experience, the bishop of Gloucester expressed the hope that the story of the crucifixion could be told to the Indigenous people, but it was pointed out to him that they knew all about crucifixion. The question was if he were able to hear about it from them. He knew about their situation in theory; they as a people had experienced abuse and murder repeatedly and the church itself had been frequently allied with the powers of evil. Rob interjected and said, "They are not the only people to be loved by Christ but rejected by the Church." Silence descended on the group. Some knew he was talking about gay people, but the Tanzanians were confused. The bishop of Western Tanganyika said, "Rob, are you talking in code? What do you mean?"

Suddenly a group of companionship and safety had become unsafe. For some, the journey was wonderful so long as ultimately all paid heed to the understanding of human sexuality articulated in Resolution I.10 of the 1998 Lambeth Conference, which said that homosexuality was incompatible with scripture and that the ordination of gay and lesbian people and the blessing of same-sex unions could not be recommended.[7] For others the journey was wonderful, but while they could endorse almost all of that same resolution, they felt it was incomplete and that in listening to the experience of gay and lesbian Christians, the resolution needed revisiting and revising. Yet others disagreed much more strongly. All was fine so long as no one talked about it; but now they all knew they that had to speak and listen.

Time was passing, and there was a need to move on within the program for that evening, so three people—one from each group—prepared a process for mutual listening the next day. Tensions were high and, especially for the bishops, this was a very stressful moment. All their work could end at this point. The next day the bishops considered simply offering a summary of teaching on human sexuality to the teams so they could focus on the day's theme of poverty and service; but the lay and ordained members resisted. The time was right to speak and listen. It was time to take a risk.

The bishop of El Camino Real quietly approached Rob and suggested that it was time to share his story with the whole group. It was time to say why he was able to cross these barriers and what motivated him in his following of Jesus.

That afternoon each of the three people who had helped prepare the process explained in turn in how gay people were viewed in their society and their church. In England, it was said that there is an increasing acceptance of gay people in society and a disconnect with Church of England practice, where their relationships were not publicly blessed. In the United States, the society is bitterly divided; The Episcopal Church is one of a relatively few religious bodies where openly gay and lesbian people could find support in a large majority of dioceses. In Tanzania, the church and society is of one mind that homosexuality is a sin, unacceptable to God and to the community. One church was out of step with its culture, another was on a "side" in a divided culture, and the third was at-one with prevailing cultural norms.

Then the room fell silent for Rob to tell his story. He spoke of the value of the friendships formed on the Indaba journey and then of the friendships formed throughout his life; how being gay had been a reality he had lived with and how he had experienced times of intense isolation in a predominantly straight society; how his identification with those who did not fit in had been his motivation in leaving well-paid jobs and offering a life of service to Jesus. What he shared was not about sex; it was about his relationship with Jesus and his total commitment to service. This commitment meant a calling to the vocational diaconate—not because his church rejected gay priests, but because it was his calling to serve the poor and the marginalized. He was called to Live Reconciliation.

As he spoke, he teared with the sadness that he would lose friends. His closest friend, Gervas, was sitting next to him and, halfway through, Gervas placed his hand on his companion's back. At that moment, Rob grew in confidence and knew that love was able to go beyond the differences in the room.

Gervas and the other Tanzanians did not "change their minds" on the legitimacy of gay unions. They were not converted by the story, but they began to understand that they had a brother, who is gay, who is also walking with Christ. The effect on others in the room was also remarkable. Rob was embraced as a brother, but so was Ken, the conservative evangelical member of the Californian team we heard from in chapter 2. He found the acceptance of the Tanzanians to be a confirmation that he could live with integrity within a diocese where most of the clergy disagreed with him, because he knew he was valued as a person.

Living Reconciliation requires us not only to see others in a different way but also to see ourselves in a new way. Often we recognize someone as "civilized" or as fully human when they most resemble ourselves, or at least the best of what we accept in ourselves.

When we stop and ask ourselves what it really means for all to speak and be heard in a community, the frustrating and time-consuming reality is almost enough to turn back to wanting one leader to set the agenda and tell us what to do! There is no quick and easy route to Living Reconciliation: it is a journey we are called to engage that redefines who we are in community and to be challenged together to grow deeper into relationships with one another and with Christ. Just as Rob,

Gervas, and Ken discovered more about themselves and the community of the three diocesan teams, we can too when we Live Reconciliation.

Jesus taking risks

In the gospels, Jesus did not entrust the leadership of the emerging church to a person who was always unquestionably right in all his judgments. Jesus trusted the pastoral care of his people to Peter, the unreliable enthusiast. Jesus knew Peter for who he was, and knew that his journey into truth and faith was in no way complete when he told him to "feed my sheep."

Jesus chose Peter, the one who was always first to volunteer and always first to fail. He was the enthusiast who would follow Jesus even when he was walking on water, and he was the failure who would immediately lose faith and start to sink. He was the man who would follow Jesus up a mountain, and the one who would misunderstand him completely. Peter is never perfect but is always discovering more. He is on a journey, constantly learning more about who Jesus is, misunderstanding what that means, and still being called to follow. It is this Peter whom Jesus calls to be a leader.

In chapter 4 we saw how Peter objected to Jesus wanting to wash his feet. Jesus calls him, and all the disciples, to a life of love and service, but Jesus knew that not all of those whose feet he washed would follow. He predicts Judas' betrayal. Peter, bouncing back from his misunderstanding and with typical zeal, reacts to Jesus' prediction by swearing absolute allegiance to Jesus. He responds by telling Peter that, before dawn, he will have denied three times the man to whom he is now swearing undying loyalty.

Jesus takes his disciples to the garden of Gethsemane and finds a quiet place to pray with Peter, James, and John. Weary and full from the Passover meal, the disciples doze off and are awakened three times by a disappointed Jesus. Three times Jesus asks them to watch with him, three times they fall asleep, and three times he wakens them. Perhaps Peter thought that his inability to stay awake was the denial Jesus had predicted. With that thought in his head, and anger at himself that he had let Jesus down, he reacts again. As Jesus is arrested, he draws his sword and cuts off the ear of the high priest's servant.

When Jesus is taken away, Peter, like the others, flees. Unlike the others, Peter quietly creeps back, following Jesus and his captors to the courtyard of the high priest's house where Jesus stands trial. Three times Peter is asked by those in the courtyard if he is in any way associated with the man on trial. Three times he fervently denies knowing Jesus. When the cock crows at the first light of the day Peter crumbles, knowing he has done what he swore he wouldn't, and has betrayed his friend.

Christians around the world read the account of Peter's denial of Jesus during Holy Week as part of what is called the Passion narrative, the story of the suffering and death of Jesus. The narrative continues with the events that follow: the trial, crucifixion, death, and resurrection of Jesus hold our focus. In order to follow this thread in Peter's journey, we will jump to one of the resurrection appearances in John's Gospel where Jesus echoes the three denials with three invitations of love and service.

At the end of John's Gospel, Jesus appears first to Mary Magdalene, then twice to the frightened disciples huddled in a locked room. The final recorded appearance is to seven of the disciples. A few days later, frustrated by the lack of action, Peter decides to go fishing and six others go with him. They fish all night and catch nothing. Just as the sun rises, a stranger on the shore tells them to cast their net again, but on the other side of the boat. When the net returns overflowing, they recognize Jesus in the abundance. Peter's reaction is typical, and he grabs his fisherman's coat, ties it around himself, leaps into the water, and races to the shore to meet Jesus, leaving the others to bring in the haul.

When the disciples get to the shore, they find Jesus sitting at a fire cooking bread and fish. He invites them to eat breakfast with him. After eating, Jesus turns to Peter and they have what, when translated into English, seems like a very strange conversation. What is translated as 'love' actually is two different Greek words that express different concepts. Jesus is asking Peter for *agape*, meaning an all-consuming, self-giving, spiritual love, which echoes the love Jesus has for the world. Peter responds with *philo*, meaning a familiar love, the love one has for a family member. Jesus' question and Peter's response are not the same. If we re-insert these meanings, we find Jesus and Peter having a very honest conversation that may have sounded a bit like this:

> *Jesus*: Simon, son of John, do you love me above and beyond all things?
>
> *Peter*: Lord, you know that I love you like a brother.
>
> *Jesus*: Simon, son of John, do you love me above all things and all people, including yourself?
>
> *Peter*: Lord you know that I love you—like a brother!
>
> *Jesus*: Simon, son of John, do you only love me as a brother?
>
> *Peter*: Lord! You know everything; and you understand that I love—as a brother.

The conversation is not an easy one. The writer of John's Gospel tells us that Peter felt hurt by Jesus' repetition and perhaps, too, the three times reminded him of his shame in denying Jesus. The writer tells us nothing of Jesus' feelings about the conversation, but this is a hard and emotional question he is asking Peter. Anyone who has ever asked another person, "Do you love me?" knows the vulnerability that it causes. Anyone who has heard the reply "Well...I *like* you" knows the crushing unevenness of feeling.

Despite the fact that Peter responds with what seems like the wrong answer, Jesus entrusts him with the ministry of serving his flock. At the end of the exchange, Jesus makes a reference to how Peter's martyrdom would glorify God, and there is almost an unspoken observation from Jesus saying: "Peter, I do understand that you only love me as a brother right now. But there is so much ahead of you and the day will come when you will be willing to give your life for my sake. Then your actions will say that you love me as I love you."

In Peter's life, this was a significant point of reconciliation. A meal with Jesus and six companions is followed by honest conversation. Being asked three times if he loved Jesus may have seemed like humiliation, but it forced him to take responsibility for his threefold failure to remain awake and his threefold denial. He is met with more than forgiveness. The reconciliation is not an end in itself; Peter now has a mission. He is to feed Jesus' sheep.

This is the story of an imperfect human being who is now sent back into the cycle of enthusiasm, ongoing failure, and reconciliation again. It is neither an end nor a beginning; it is part of the flow of his relationship with God, Father, Son, and Spirit.

Everyday risk

Living Reconciliation means living with the joy and tension of hope. Hope drives us on to seek for more truth. It encourages us toward justice. But hope in the return of Christ makes us realistic about the sense of not being complete in the present.

Points of reconciliation on the journey are never the end of the story; they are markers on the way.

Abraham's acceptance of his son Ishmael did not solve the problem. The Church of England did not find a solution to the contradictions in the varying interpretations of scripture, tradition, and reason over female bishops, even within the facilitated conversations in its General Synod. Peter remained the reckless enthusiast who was liable to fall flat on his face. Living Reconciliation is not about "happy ever after" endings. Living Reconciliation is the mission of the Church, the constant requirement for forgiveness, and belonging in a community of people who value uniqueness. Living Reconciliation means living with imperfection.

In order for us to be energized within this messy world we need hope and we need that hope to be based on a firm foundation. The foundation of hope is in God and is seen in the life, death, and resurrection of Jesus.

* * *

Prayer

> Loving God, who spoke the world into being and invites us into conversation, teach us to listen with love and speak with boldness, that together we might hear your voice in our world. *Amen.*

Questions to think about

1. How does the conversation between Jesus and Peter help us to have similar conversations?

2. Do you know anyone who is loved by Christ but rejected by the Church?

3. When have you taken a risk in order to follow Christ?

Further thinking

For additional material on the topics discussed in this chapter—including videos, study guides, and further reading—please visit www.living-reconciliation.org.

Chapter 7

New way of being

Paul's letter to the Philippians was a communication between Paul and a church that he regarded as healthy. The relationship between Paul and his community in Rome and the Christians of Philippi is one of partnership and, unlike other letters such as those to the Corinthians, he is not writing out of anger or concern. It is as a model of how communities can learn to Live Reconciliation.

This does not mean that either Paul's own community or that in Philippi was perfect. They were not. In Paul's own community, people acted with pride and selfish ambition, and the Philippians had arguments and rivalries of their own. However, both communities were struggling to remain faithful and were working out how to live in obedience to Christ, the great reconciler. The evidence of their struggle is found within the letter Paul wrote to them and this is why it is such a significant guide for us as we seek to do the same.

Philippians 2:3–11 underpins everything written in the letter to the Philippians, revealing the central core of the life of reconciliation—Christ himself.

Do nothing from selfish ambition or conceit, but in humility regard others as better than yourselves. Let each of you look not to your own interests, but to the interests of others. Let the same mind be in you that was in Christ Jesus, who, though he was in the form of God, did not regard equality with God as something to be exploited, but emptied himself, taking the form of a slave, being born in human likeness. And being found in human form, he humbled himself and became obedient to the point of death— even death on a cross.

Therefore God also highly exalted him and gave him the name that is above every name, so that at the name of Jesus every knee should bend, in heaven and on earth and under the earth, and every tongue should confess that Jesus Christ is Lord, to the glory of God the Father.

At the core of this passage is a hymn of praise to Christ the reconciler, but look at how Paul uses the hymn. He does not unpack the theology of incarnation; he calls on the Philippian community to live in the way of Christ. It is not enough just to understand the reconciliation story; it is vital to live it.

Reading scripture and worshiping together was one of Paul's pieces of advice to the Philippians. It is important for us too, and it grounds our relationships with one another in the all-encompassing love of God.

Living Reconciliation begins with an openness to share in the lives of our companions. This starts with the sharing of hospitality, and a commitment to listening and to speaking together. Through this, relationships are formed where honest conversations and disagreements can happen. It is vital that we form relationships so that there is a safe space to take risks together.

Honest hospitality

A starting point is to share hospitality. As you read through the gospels, it may have struck you how many times shared meals are mentioned. Jesus appears to move from meal to meal. Preaching is effective with large numbers, but it is in the intimate encounters that Jesus is able to talk about being born again to Nicodemus and to engage in conversation with Mary while her sister Martha is in the kitchen. Jesus' radical love overcame barriers to hospitality and relationship, which is shown by how he eats with all kinds of people—many of whom his culture dictated that he should not have socialized with. The gospel-writers' accounts of these personal conversations point to how serious they are. Relationships are developed over a meal, giving rise to conversations that change people. Often Jesus is the guest, invited in as he was by the walkers to Emmaus. In other cases, such as the final supper or the meal by the lake following his resurrection, he is the host. The receiving and giving of hospitality is a vital element in developing the relationships that are essential in Living Reconciliation.

As churches, we are far more comfortable in being the host than the guest. We like to invite people into our world. We invite people to eat with us as part of our Alpha courses, and we invite them to sing with us at Christmas. We set up signs saying that all are welcome, and we encourage people visiting on special Sundays to come back. Our default mission direction is to invite people in. However, the history of Christian mission shows us that successful evangelism has usually relied on Christians going out. Transformation has occurred when the people of God go out and accept the hospitality of the community. This was what Jesus told the seventy-two to do in Luke 10:1–23.

There is a popular image of Paul the tentmaker setting up camp in town after town, inviting people to listen to him on his terms. While this may have happened from time to time, Acts 16 tells us that in Philippi he shared in the hospitality of a local dealer in purple cloth. Lydia persuades Paul to stay with her and her family in her home after hearing him speak. This was the beginning of the church that Paul regarded as the most faithful of all those we know to which he wrote.

The first step of reconciliation is to step out of our comfort zone and experience the hospitality offered to us. However much effort we put into making our places friendly, inviting others into our place of security puts the power in our hands. Just as Jesus stepped into our world with every possibility of rejection, those who Live Reconciliation need to step outside and be the ones who experience discomfort. Paul's first encounter in Europe was at a meeting of women where, as a man, he may have felt entirely out of place. In accepting the invitation to the home of a woman, he may have been vulnerable to all kinds of rumor and scandal. Regardless, he accepted the invitation and the foundations of a reconciled and reconciling community were laid.

Receiving hospitality in someone else's place is the first step in breaking down barriers. However, it is not easy. It also must take place in a way that people are unlikely to be harmed or made to feel unsafe. The hardest part of designing the Continuing Indaba pilot conversations, though, was in convincing the teams to open their own homes to one another and offer hospitality. They believed that they were being far better hosts by arranging for hotels.

When two members of the New York team designed their own diocesan Indaba, they made staying in one another's homes a requirement. They did this because they knew that the most significant points of transformation had come in the homes they had visited. But many people were reticent and saw this as an imposition. However, the design team knew from their experience that staying in people's homes is where conversation moved from formal to informal, artificial to real. During the New York Indaba, they spent Saturday evenings in the home of someone on the same journey. They ate with their families, talking and simply being with one another. It wasn't optional; it was the process. Relationships began to grow and barriers that the diocese had used to define different groups—poor and rich, rural and metropolitan—became less important.

In chapter 3, we described a dilemma when a delegation approached a rector complaining that they only wanted to worship on Sunday morning with those they partied with on Saturday night. The vicar's indignation was understandable, but in a way they were right—not about who they were excluding on a Sunday morning, but about who they were excluding at their social gatherings. They needed to be partying with those of diverse social standings if they were to be a true community of reconciliation. A community of reconciliation has to overcome the discomfort of being host and visitor across all kinds of social barriers.

The first Christian communities did not have any special buildings; they met in one another's homes. This was the ideal of the early Christians recorded in Acts 2:42. However, there were problems in some of the early churches that became obvious in Corinth where the divisions over social exclusion were at the heart of the conflict in the Christian community. The divided Corinthian groups were not building rival chapels;

they were meeting in different homes. Their divisions resulted in direct discrimination. When Paul writes to the Corinthian church about how the Lord's Supper should be done, it was because this was an actual meal in people's homes and the poor and slaves were being socially excluded. Paul challenges the community in Corinth to go beyond the barriers of social exclusion and be a community of believers remembering Christ's death and resurrection.

Centuries of history have led us to make our eucharistic celebration a distinct act separate from the eating of a meal, but the liturgies we use still resound with the imagery of hospitality. People are welcomed and invited as they move from pew to table. They are asked to reconcile with God in confession and hear the scriptures read and considered in a communal context before performing a symbolic act of reconciliation. The Eucharistic Prayer recalls that Jesus was at a meal with his disciples when he blessed the bread and the wine. But more than that, it recalls the central act of reconciliation before it is declared that "though we are many we are one because we all eat of the one bread and drink from the one cup." The ending is just as significant. The modern liturgy ends not with a blessing but with a commissioning; the congregation is sent out to love and serve.

The eucharistic liturgy is a challenge as well as a blessing. If we take it seriously, then the words and actions are there to melt the walls of the very buildings that hold its beauty. Great care has been taken to honor God in the development of architecture.

Some of our buildings are awe-inspiring in the way that they speak of the greatness of God. But the eucharist speaks of hospitality shared, and we can focus so much on inviting people in that we forget that the direction of the liturgy is in sending people out. The very word 'Mass' is derived from the same source as mission—a word that sends out.

A church community that takes the eucharist seriously is one that seeks to understand church as having porous walls. If the church is the people, we need to be the church inside and outside of the building. This means we are being commissioned to share hospitality with all. Church is not just a place you invite others into; it is a community of people who accept invitations as well as give them out. It is only when we are able to be guests that we can be hosts.

There has been much written in the last few years on the idea of radical hospitality as a way of being church. Congregations are encouraged to develop the desire to invite, welcome, receive, and care for those who are strangers. It is about going the extra mile, going beyond what is expected of us in society, and giving without counting the cost. This is important—to welcome others as we would welcome Christ. However, hospitality is so much more. Hospitality is not a one-way action; it is a cycle, a cycle of giving and receiving, a cycle of love. It is a place in which we welcome the other as Christ, but also a place where we allow ourselves to be welcomed as Christ. Hospitality is the action that leads to shared power.

Welcoming someone into your home is to welcome them into your life. Some people dislike this idea. Some fear that our homes aren't good enough, that we will be judged on the state of our housekeeping, or that the books or DVDs on our shelves will not be up to guests' expectations. Others fear they will appear to be showing off their wealth and social status. When we overcome these fears, we find ourselves relaxing with friends rather than welcoming strangers.

In ancient Celtic society, hospitality was a way of life and anyone who was offered hospitality came under the protection of the host. Hospitality was seen as having a threefold nature: giving, receiving, and meeting Christ in one another. This is the cycle of Living Reconciliation, where we learn to give and receive hospitality and learn to see Christ in those who are different from us. Richard Kerr, a Presbyterian minister in Belfast, wrote an engaging and challenging article on what it meant to follow Christ and welcome refugees and asylum seekers in Northern Ireland. In "Embracing the Stranger," Kerr unpacks both Jesus' call and the example he set for his followers to offer hospitality to strangers as central to their lives:

> His great call is to hospitality, a central theme of scripture. Jesus epitomized hospitality in his welcome and treatment of those on the fringes of society. But it was more than a welcome. His hospitality was about reconciliation and the transformation from stranger to guest and from guest to friend.[1]

As Kerr says, Jesus is not calling us to host dinner parties and to be nice to the new people who walk into church for the first time. Hospitality is about reconciliation, transformation, and journeying on together. It is about challenging the boundaries that include some and exclude others.

In 2011 there were riots in several towns in the United Kingdom. In Birmingham, three young Muslim boys were run down by a car in what was perceived to be an inter-ethnic attack that could have led to cycles of recurring violence. The father of one of the boys made public appeals for calm and reconciliation. At the first opportunity, two Christian leaders—one ordained and one lay—accepted an invitation to attend an open act of reconciliation in a city park. What is remembered in the Muslim community is that the Rev. Rana Khan, wearing his clergy collar, came and prayed with them. He was marked as a Christian minister, but he bowed to pray in the manner of the whole community. He prayed among them and with them, accepting the vulnerability of being a Christian embracing their form of prayer. He was not there to judge, but to participate and to learn from their gestures of reconciliation. Their invitation and his response were vital for the reconciliation process.

A year later Rana Khan received an invitation to preach during Friday prayers at an important mosque in Luton—a town known for the radicalization of young Muslims embracing jihad. He was invited to preach as a Christian, wearing his cassock, and to speak of reconciliation. Could a Muslim be offered the same opportunity in our churches? The cycle of hospitality is the first step in Living Reconciliation. Are we prepared to take the step?

Hearing and being heard

Sharing hospitality changes the relationship of power between people and creates the context for reconciliation. Being able to enter into one another's space, we accept vulnerability and step beyond animosity into relationship. But this is only a beginning; a further step is the need to hear and to be heard.

Paul continued his journey from Philippi through Macedonia to the heart of European culture, Athens. He was distressed by the idols that decorated the city, and it would have been easy for him to have condemned them outright. But he listened instead, learning the culture and discovering its prevailing world-view. When the invitation came for him to speak in the public forum, he did so with respect and recognition that he was learning as well as having something to offer. Commenting on Paul in Athens, Ugandan former bishop and anti-corruption activist Zac Niringiye says:

> Every culture and epoch in history has within it signs, pointing to his presence among them. But there is more to listening and dialogue: since the good news is about the Kingdom of God in creation, proclamation is rooted in the

conviction that every culture has within it the capacity not only to receive the good news but to be a transmitter.[2]

Writing a hundred years ago, Roland Allen contrasted Paul's approach to that of the missionaries of his own generation who in their racial and religious pride approached the "heathen" as if they were superior beings "moved by charity to impart of our wealth to destitute and perishing souls."[3] He argued that Paul entered communities with respect, listening, and learning as well as speaking. Paul was heard because of the respect he showed in listening. Allen called on missionaries to use Paul's methods.

The Coventry Cathedral's approach to reconciliation begins with "healing the wounds of history." These wounds are only healed if history is spoken and heard from all perspectives. Therefore, the practice of listening is a vital element of that reconciliation. When we are in the midst of a conflict, the desire to correct the other person's view of history can be overwhelming. We can see this in televised debates between political opponents. Each one is listening attentively to the other, but only to find ammunition in order to score points. Listening for reconciliation requires a different intention and different skills.

The intention of listening for reconciliation is to hear the other with an openness that can discover the depth of their humanity. It is not to find counter arguments, but to come to know the person better. In a debate, by contrast, the speaker aims to highlight powerful points and convince those who might be inclined to join that side. In Living Reconciliation the intention of speaking is to share truth, but also to articulate unknowing: the speaker is open to discovering more of the truth. Sometimes this occurs in regular conversation as part of our everyday experience of community life. At other times, it is especially important to create the space for such conversations and to use processes that allow people to hear and be heard.

Sometimes we may think we know someone so well that we assume what they are going say and we don't indicate that we really want to listen. If tension or conflict is present, deep listening is even more difficult. In marriage therapy, it can be helpful for both spouses to share their perspectives and grievances. A method used by counselors is to have one partner speak their truth for two minutes, with no interruptions. The spouse is then asked to give a thirty-second summary that can be corrected and clarified by the speaker. The same process is then repeated by the other person. A single incident or a habitual event can be seen in a very different light by two people who share a common life. This process can be transformational for both the individuals and their marriage. In our communities, the use of intentional methods for listening and speaking can be equally significant. There are many such processes that can be useful, and some will work for nearly any group. Healing the wounds of history sounds very simple, but it involves opening up and hearing deep pain.

Conversations are made more complex when those speaking are also thinking in different languages. Communication barriers are not overcome simply by translation. Languages reflect the cultural perspectives of the community out of which they emerge. Although translation can help, the way of thinking can be very different. Careful listening requires entering into another world-view and using the skills we looked at in chapter 3.

In some ways, conversations between people of differing world-views who share the same language can be even more challenging. The same English word may not have a common meaning to people of a different generation, let alone when used by people from Australia, the United Kingdom, the United States, Canada, or elsewhere. Even when differences in the use of vocabulary are accounted for, the assumptions that underlie the reasoning may need to be unpacked. Sometimes there is need for a facilitator.

Facilitation

It may come as a surprise to many that we have progressed so far into a book on reconciliation without looking at the role of facilitators. There is a myth that great facilitators can solve all problems; they can't. Facilitators can work with people who are seeking to hear and be heard, and can help them to see what is blocking their desire to reconcile. Facilitators can help make deep conversation possible when the participants are ready to trust them and work with them.

Facilitation is not a new idea. In Philippians 4 we read about two leaders within the Philippian community who were involved in a deep conflict, and Paul reaches out to a facilitator. Euodia and Syntyche were both established members of the church in Philippi. Paul knew them well as women who had worked side by side with him for the gospel and "had their names written in the book of life." But they were barely talking to one another. Paul asked a faithful companion to act as a facilitator to help them to talk to one another. In the end, the success or failure of the process was in their hands, but the desire to establish an intentional way of making conversation possible was vital. This is the case today. Facilitators have very special skills and abilities that should be nurtured and valued. But in the end, the responsibility for listening and speaking rests with all of us.

For years a group of women passionate to see social transformation had been meeting in New York. Half were from the United States and half from Africa. They all were completely committed to alleviating poverty, fighting injustice, and ending violence toward women and girls. Year after year they reported having a meaningful time, but they also reported a growing frustration that hoped-for outcomes were not being realized. They called for assistance from Continuing Indaba. Two experienced facilitators began to work with them. Their work began months before the meeting, learning about the group, and discussing aims and objectives. One facilitator was from Africa and the other from North America. This was vital. Both were able to step from one culture into another, but in combination they were able to pick up the cultural messages set out by the women from their own culture in a way that would be impossible otherwise.

The facilitators picked up on all kinds of cultural concerns that had been blocking the conversation. The African women had no idea that violence toward women and girls was a problem in the United States; they thought it was just their problem. The facilitators identified the imbalance in power within the group and relieved the American participants of a felt need to teach. They also encouraged them to suspend their own cultural norms for communication in order to engage in earnest and patient listening to their African counterparts. The Americans gave space for the African participants to take risks and speak openly to a group of women they barely knew. The result was transformational. The African women began to share competencies and ideas for social transformation with one another and with the Americans. The opportunity for all to go out to Live Reconciliation was made possible through skillful facilitation.

Worship and prayer together

As we saw from Rana's story, praying together is a vital and powerful step in reconciliation. When we begin a journey of reconciliation, we might not even be able to imagine praying with one another—although we might be praying for one another. Just as we need to share the hospitality of our homes with one another, we need to share the hospitality of our churches.

The Anglican Communion itself is blessed with a rich diversity of ways in which the people of God praise and receive from God—Father, Son, and Holy Spirit. This in itself has been a cause of conflict in our history. However, praying and worshiping together are vital for a Christian community to grow together.

If we are trying to Live Reconciliation within a church community or between church communities, then knowing how we each encounter God is vital. Just as sharing the hospitality of our homes is important, so is sharing the hospitality of our churches; not just in swapping preachers or priests, but in genuinely discovering how your companions worship. If some use the angelus but others see this as idolatry, or if some value loud music and others crave silence, then it is vital to engage with one another and seek to understand why that form of worship moves them. It is important to share usual worship methods with one another. Don't avoid something because it might cause offense, but also don't do things that you usually wouldn't do just to annoy companions! Finding ways to worship God genuinely in an alien context can be difficult, but engaging together deepens relationships with God and one another.

Reading scripture together

There can be real fear over reading scripture with those who disagree with us. We may fear that going over old differences will shut down conversation or lead us into a bitter argument. But it is important to understand how our companions understand scripture before we focus on passages that might prove to be controversial. Using the lectionary readings rather than choosing a reading to impose on one another can be helpful as we begin to listen to how scripture is part of our faith journeys. No matter what our liturgical tradition in the Anglican Communion, the Word of God is central to our worship and our lives as Christians; but we don't all understand scripture in the same way. Many things can influence the way we read and interpret scripture. The structures of our families; whether we are rich, poor, or somewhere in between; what education we have received; and if we come from places where there are separations in society based on gender, race, ethnicity, or class; all of these things, and many more, affect our relationship with the Bible. When we read scripture together with openness to understanding one another's contexts, we understand better their perspectives. Often, engaging openly in our own relationship with scripture and context creates space for deeper understanding to emerge.

Sometimes those who have studied scripture academically can dominate the voices of those whose experience of scripture comes out of their daily lives. The Rev. Mote Magomba, a priest in the Anglican Church of Tanzania, explored this idea in his article "The Bible and Polygamy in Tanzania." He discusses the conflict between what he calls "ordinary readers" and "academic readers" of the Bible, using a Tanzanian story to illustrate what he means by "ordinary" readers:

> A village woman used to walk around always carrying her Bible. "Why always the Bible?" her neighbors asked teasingly. "There are so many books you can read." The woman knelt down, held the Bible above her head and said, "Yes, of course there are many books which I could read. But there is only one book which reads me." The Tanzanian village woman has seen and understood the mystery of the Bible, that it is not just the object of our study and interpretation; it is the subject who understands us better than we do ourselves.[4]

Magomba explores the idea that "ordinary readers" of the Bible are not just recipients of academic interpretation; they are creatively appropriating biblical texts and applying them to their lives. He doesn't suggest that academic readings are not important, but that a complimentary model of reading scripture would be more enriching to all than a model where one view has dominance over the other.

During the Continuing Indaba pilot project, a form of *lectio divina* was an important tool because of its emphasis on all voices being heard and all insights valued. *Lectio* is an ancient way of exploring the scriptures together that has been practiced by Christians from the sixth century onward. It involves reading, reflecting, listening, sharing, and praying. A form of *lectio*, introduced by the Southern African delegation to the Lambeth Conference in 2008, has been used throughout Continuing Indaba. The aim is to open us up to God's word together and to enable us to respond to God in prayer.

The choice of which scripture to study is very significant. A text that minimizes difference can offer an illusion of tolerance, while one that requires a deep understanding of culture could place power in the hands of the more educated. A text that is deeply contentious can lead to prepared speeches taking over the process. When making a major decision, Indigenous Anglicans in Canada used a modified version of *lectio*, reading and rereading the texts over a long period of time. They chose to use the lectionary readings. To everyone's surprise, those attending meeting after meeting over a period of months spoke with one accord about how the texts had transformed the conversation even though none were directly relevant to the issue at-hand. It is always important for the scriptures themselves to be center stage, rather than the choice of scripture.

Imagine what it might mean for the church if we all came to acknowledge one another as equal partners in a joint enterprise and worked together in reading the Bible. Imagine what it would mean to read scripture as part of a faith journey together, from many perspectives.

African or Lambeth *lectio*

This form of *lectio* was used throughout the Continuing Indaba conversations, as it allowed time for speaking and listening to one another and to God.

Opening Prayer:

> O Blessed Lord, who caused all Holy Scripture to be written for our learning: Grant us so to hear them, read, mark, learn, and inwardly digest them, that we may embrace and hold fast the blessed hope of everlasting life, which you have given us in our savior Jesus Christ, *Amen*.

One individual reads passages slowly.

Each person identifies the word or phrase that catches their attention. (1 minute)

Each shares the word or phrase around the group. (3–5 minutes, no discussion)

Another person reads the passage slowly (from a different translation, if possible).

Each person identifies where this passage touches their life today. (1 minute)

Each shares. (3–5 minutes, no discussion)

Passage is read a third time (another reader and translation, if possible. Or even another language).

Each person names or writes: "From what I've heard and shared, what do I believe God wants me to do or be? Is God inviting me to change in any way?" (5 minutes)

Each shares their answer. (5–10 minutes, no discussion)

Each prays for the person on their right, naming what was shared in other steps. (5 minutes)

Close with the Lord's Prayer and silence.

New way of being

The sense of community shines through the communication between Paul and the Philippians. Although he had founded their church, he did not set himself up as their superior, stressing instead his status as a slave of Christ. They were his sponsors, sending him money, but in his thanks to them, he celebrated by giving glory to God and retaining his independence. The relationship was founded on mutual hospitality. Paul had lived in Lydia's house; their representative,

Epaphroditus, was living with Paul. They were committed to ongoing communication, and when there was a conflict they were prepared to use facilitation. The hymn of praise to Jesus was not just a doctrinal statement, but one that was expected to shape behavior and be lived in community.

As your community Lives Reconciliation in this way, you will begin to see barriers come down and both your church and your world being transformed. The stories in the next chapter offer that new vision of hope.

* * *

Prayer

> Loving God, who chose the hospitality of a virgin's womb and who feeds us with your very self, give us the mind of Christ to welcome one another as we would welcome you. *Amen.*

Questions to think about

1. Do you think evangelism is more effective if you go out to the community or bring people into your context? Is this different if the context is local, cross-cultural, or international?

2. How do the Philippian hymn and the stories of hospitality help us think about what it means to be host and guest?

3. Do we recognize and welcome Christ in one another? How do you feel when the Christ in you is welcomed?

Further thinking

For additional material on the topics discussed in this chapter—including videos, study guides, and further reading—please visit www.living-reconciliation.org.

Chapter 8

Sharing the vision

Central California is a beautiful place to live. The town of Monterey nestles onto a rugged coastline that attracts millions of visitors every year. As tourists meander along the world famous seventeen-mile drive, they pass by exclusive championship golf courses and gaze onto the azure ocean, frolicking sea otters, and basking sea lions. To the north, Silicon Valley is home to the most creative and productive multinational companies such as Google, Facebook, Apple, and eBay. Their employees work in environments designed for them to enjoy every moment of their day. It is an especially fine place to be healthy and wealthy.

Life is completely different in the rural heartlands just off the tourist routes. The region is a center for industrialized farming, providing fruit and vegetables to other parts of the United States and for export elsewhere—an industry that relies on large numbers of low-income temporary workers. The county of Monterey also can be a deadly place to live. It is home to a multitude of youth gangs and has one of the highest youth homicide rates in the country. In some schools, administrators patrol the fences dividing playgrounds that separate young people who might otherwise take violent revenge for perceived insults. The chief of police in the Salinas Valley says that he has never met a hopeful gang member. Gangs become communities defined by fear, and this manifests itself in aggression.

The rural gang culture is in the midst of the Diocese of El Camino Real, which spans from Monterey to Silicon Valley. The diocese is committed to Living Reconciliation not because of its participation in the Continuing Indaba program, but because of the leadership of its people, lay and ordained, as well as Bishop Mary Gray-Reeves. This commitment to Living Reconciliation has made the diocese a significant force in Anglican Communion reconciliation. It is the same commitment that places the diocese at the heart of making a difference in the gang culture. Deacon Rob Sommer, whom we met in chapter 6, plays a central role in its involvement with gangs. His experience of crossing cultural barriers makes him a vital catalyst in the community, and he is making a genuine difference in the lives of the young people.

The New Testament speaks of communities of belonging, of being a family. But compared to gang culture, this gospel community is based on hope not fear, openness not insularity. The desire for genuine community lives in the hearts and souls of the people, and Rob helps them to draw upon their own resources to change their world. His ministry has been called a "youth ministry," but it isn't; it is a ministry to families, reconnecting youth to the whole community. It has been called "gang prevention," but it isn't; it is about focusing the desire for community away from violence and toward peace.

Rob emphasizes that community organizing will work only if it is done *with* and not *for* the youth, so that together they create an environment of hope. They use football teams to build up belonging; they provide access to computers, put on art shows, and clean up beaches. It matters less what activities are actually done so long as the energy for action comes from within the community itself and so long as it builds mutual confidence. The churches' role is vital, but only if they are living out the gospel in the community and not telling the community what to do.

The church can play a vital role in helping communication take place by offering space for conversation, but only if it is "out there" in the community, and not expecting young people to come inside its doors. Rob stresses ideas such as partnering with all interested groups in working with young people, including other denominations. The support of the bishop of El Camino Real has been central in establishing a ministry that is not defined by parish and Sunday morning. She also has been vital in establishing links to the other denominations that have influence in the region, especially the Roman Catholic Church.

Rob is a person transformed by Living Reconciliation, serving in a diocese that is defined by a commitment to reconciliation.

This is lived out at many levels at the same time; not only in its mission in a local context, but also in how it has built bridges between congregations that have very different theological perspectives. This commitment is lived out through its ecumenical relationships locally and through its commitment to the Anglican Communion. The diocese has seen its bishop take a lead in building relationships across barriers that seemed unbreakable.

This is the holistic nature of Living Reconciliation. The Holy Spirit infuses us with hope for a new future, and as we imagine that future we become agents of transformation in our world and in the church. If we work on reconciliation in our church communities, we will break down the barriers that separate our church from the world. It is not possible to work for reconciliation in divided communities if we are not living it in our church.

In this final chapter, we will visit some dioceses and parishes where they are Living Reconciliation in the church and the world. We will highlight some of the key actions they took in order to turn aspiration into action and the reasons for their enthusiasm.

Indaba inspiration

Living Reconciliation is not just an aspiration; it also needs inspiration. For the Diocese of Saldanha Bay (South Africa), participation in the Continuing Indaba pilot conversations was revolutionary. The diocesan team discovered what they described as a "new way of being," and Bishop Raphael Hess was keen to share this with the entire diocese.

Bishop Hess had a desire for "Indaba to infiltrate and infect diocesan meetings," but he had questions about how to get those on key committees of the diocese to catch the vision.[1] As South Africans, they were familiar with the concept of Indaba as a community process for discernment on matters of significance. The challenge was how that understanding might affect the church structures they had inherited from the Church of England and colonialism. These would have to be transformed if they were going to live a new way—to Live Reconciliation.

The first task for those proposing a change in the way of being church is to *communicate clearly the need for change* and to signify how it will further the key aims of the community. In this case energy for change came from the bishop, but in other cases it has come from lay and ordained members of a community.

When Bishop Hess approached those who were in positions of responsibility within the diocese, they argued whether constitutional procedure could be replaced by Indaba. They came to the decision that both were vital for good decision-making. They also realized that the members of the Board of Finance, the Diocesan Chapter, and others first needed to own the process and understand how it changed the priorities of the diocese.

Leadership that reflects these principles, according to Bishop Hess, is slower, more patient, aware of its own inadequacies, is consultative, and is willing to take risks. This is reflected in the way he works with the diocese, sharing power, and bringing in the necessary skills and voices. Collaborative leadership needs to be inclusive, he says, which means slowing down and asking who needs to be present, and who is not being heard. Indaba, for him, is something to which all come on equal footing. It is when perceived and real power are consciously and genuinely relinquished, and people feel like it is shared, that all feel "in this together."

Bishop Hess is mirroring servant leadership. This is leadership that gains authority without embracing dominating power. The first task of leaders in encouraging their people to Live Reconciliation is to make sure that it is owned by their community. The key shift is from top-down, decision-making to consensual decision-making. The community is then challenged to take responsibility and care for one another. It's worth noting that all are part of the community, and this includes the leaders!

Living Reconciliation begins when a community starts to work out what it means to imitate Christ together. All are to place the interests of others first and to listen to one another, working out what it means to obey Christ together in their contexts. This is the foundation of a community Living

Reconciliation. It is a *new way of being with one another* that breathes life into communities, allows space for all voices, and takes risks together.

If the first task is to communicate the need for a new way, the second is for *leadership that places trust in God and in the community*. The community needs to hear that they are trusted to discover where God is calling them, and that leaders relinquish the power to decide outcomes.

This is what Paul calls for in Philippians. If we look again at the text of Philippians 2, the verses before the great hymn say that the reconciled community is founded on humility. In the verses that follow it, there is a call to obey Christ and to "continue to work out our own salvation with fear and trembling."[2] In Paul's understanding, being obedient to Christ is not about following a predetermined set of rules; it's about living under the lordship of Christ in community. This is why, according to Bible commentator Gordon Fee, Paul says they need to work out their own salvation. Fee argues that this does not mean an exploration of the theology of salvation, or living out the gospel through works. He points out that understanding what obedience to Christ means is worked out in community, not individually.[3] Paul is asking them to work together on the implications of the gospel. It is not his role and not the role of elders to do this alone; it is participatory. We all have a part to play.

In Paul's understanding, obedience to Christ is developed through maturity, and maturity comes from taking responsibility.

Remaining as children leaves us open to being blown about by the whims and fashions of those who speak with loud, forceful voices.

Leadership that inspires is vital in building a mature community of faith. Paul continually reminded the communities he wrote to about the core message of the gospel, and he trusted them with the task of making it real in their lives. Great leadership empowers all.

Setting the agenda, designing the process

Many communities across the Anglican Communion are very familiar with consensual processes for decision-making; it's important for us to learn from them. One community where Living Reconciliation comes naturally is among the Indigenous Anglicans in Canada.

In 2008 a small committee of Indigenous Canadian Anglicans were asked to consider a revolutionary church structure. In order to consider the proposal, they gathered in "sacred circles" to allow all voices to be heard. The process seemed drawn-out and wandering to many outsiders. It involved reflecting on scripture and singing songs that may have looked like avoiding the question. In 2014 the process is drawing to a close, six long years after it started, but it has produced a result that is consensual and effective. Not all agree, but all agree on a way forward that respects the diversity and difference within the community. "Quicker" and seemingly more "efficient" processes of decision-making can result in divided communities and a minority group refusing to accept change even when it has the approval of a synod or convention.

The Indigenous Anglicans offer two key lessons: they had a framing question and they had a designed process. For them the agenda was set by an official body of the Anglican Church of Canada, and the process emerged from work that had been established through a long period of time. In other contexts, it will not be as simple.

The focus for *a framing question* should be a matter that concerns the community and is relevant to all. Framing questions should be short, specific, and focused. They should be open questions, inviting dialogue. Effective questions might be "What is the nature of our common life?" or "How can we become a church that includes people of all generations?" They are often the most important questions that a church community can ask.

It is vital to *design the process* intentionally, whether it's to take place within a governance setting or as a stand-alone journey. The leader or convenor has the responsibility to appoint the design group. Although members may be recommended by others, they all need to know that they have the trust of the leader.

Since there are both advantages and disadvantages for the recognized leader—such as the bishop or the rector—being on the design group, these need to be considered. Groups will behave differently in the leader's presence; leaders also may be unaware of the effect they have on groups. They can, unintentionally, shut down voices, as members seek to conform to the wishes of the most powerful person. It is hard to retain authority and create a setting where power is shared. However, if the leader is not present, the group will fear making decisions that might not be supported. In addition the group will need to ask the leader practical questions, sometimes as simple as a scheduling date that needs to be confirmed.

It is usually best for the leader or convenor not to be on the design group, but for someone to chair it who is trusted by both the convenor and the group, and who is in clear communication with the convenor. Good communication is important. When the group requires an answer, or for something to happen, the chair needs to know that he or she can speak directly with the convenor, who will listen, and that the convenor will trust the design group. The design group also will need the convenor to support its decisions when potential participants are questioning vital aspects of the design.

New York

New York is the one place in the world where processes of Living Reconciliation should be the most difficult. If it can be done there, it can be done anywhere. The New York culture is one of a quick fix, of instant solutions; it's a place where problems are solved by powerful people. In 2013 the incoming diocesan bishop had an advantage. Bishop Andrew Dietsche had served in the diocese for many years, knew every parish, and had a grasp of all the issues. A year serving alongside his predecessor had allowed him to listen to people expressing concerns on funding and parish viability everywhere he went. The expectation was that he would fix the problems immediately.

Bishop Dietsche took a different approach. In the sermon at his installation, he called on the diocese to begin "a diocesan-wide conversation under the rubric of Indaba."[4] He then set out the framing question:

> If as I believe the world desperately needs the church to be the church, what does that mean for us in the places where we are and in the contexts in which God has planted us? What does it mean to be the church? What and who are we? What is this strange unworldly calling, when we are compelled to be the church and what are those things which God requires of us which only we can do?[5]

He was later to refine the focus, asking those participating to gain "a shared understanding of our common life."[6]

The bishop had envisioned the Indaba being completed in 2013. He had thought that they could just get it done; but when he appointed a design team, he discovered that it would take a lot longer and require a great deal of energy and commitment.

The New York design team was effective because it was small and focused, and also because it had people within it who understood both the principles and practicalities that would make or break the journey. Whatever process is undertaken, it has to be owned and designed by the people who are going to be involved.

Nothing about us without us

In most places across the world, the decision-making bodies are dominated by people whose hair is graying or disappearing. They are well aware of their distance from young people. When they want to address youth issues, the first temptation is to invite youth workers as advocates to their boards, committees, or synods, where they are asked to present policies and action plans. In some places this may be supplemented by inviting youth representatives onto the vestry, church or diocesan council, or inviting the occasional youth delegation to speak. Such processes have a very limited effect.

The youth of the Diocese of Saldanha Bay designed their own process, inviting participation from the wider Church. For them there could be no decision on their inclusion without their full participation. The change in power, from the decision-making body inviting youth to the youth inviting those representing the church structures, is an example of the radical change required. If the focus is on youth, then young people need to be involved.

The members of the design group must be able to ensure that *design of the process is inclusive*. If the framing question is about an ethnic conflict, people from all sides must be present in developing the design. If the focus—as in New York—is between the conflicting interests of urban and rural, rich and poor, then the design needs to include all of these voices.

Challenging structures

Bishop Alan Scarfe of Iowa was invited to the diocesan synod of his link diocese in South Sudan by Bishop Samuel Peni. He expected it to be similar to the diocesan conventions of his church, or the synods of churches such as the Anglican Church of Canada or the Church of England. What he found, instead, was a group of people who addressed one another directly. They did not polarize themselves into groups for and against a motion, and they came to a conclusion without requiring a formal resolution. The Sudanese church regularly uses Indaba-style methods when facing critical questions. At an Anglican gathering, Bishop Enoch Tombe from South Sudan said that they always use traditional methods from their own local communities when the church forum fails to address an issue that particularly relates to local culture. Bishop Scarfe was amazed, and he saw the potential.

The challenge was how he might transfer such processes to the structures of his own church. Leaders cannot impose consensual methods on a community; they have to be owned and supported by all, and communities can be very resistant to change. He used diocesan news outlets to introduce the idea that there could be a change in diocesan process. He talked it through with key powerful leaders, and he invited members of his diocesan convention to taste and see.

It was at this point that power began to be shared. The diocesan conventions in most Episcopal Church dioceses take place in large halls with delegates seated around circular tables. As parish delegates arrive, they may mark out their territory with mascots or candies in the middle of the table. The bigger parishes have a table of their own, with the smaller parishes sharing tables. As a trial, the design team assigned delegates to different tables, breaking up the usual pattern. The plan was for them to consider a minor issue and then return to the normal pattern for business as usual, before reflecting on how they might proceed in the future.

What the bishop had not expected was the delegates' eagerness to go beyond his limited objectives. In his opening address, as well as in setting out the process for the Indaba groups, he raised an issue of deep concern. But the delegates asked that the Indaba session might focus on the difficult and significant issue rather than something they saw as less important. Asking for the space to "work out their own salvation," they took responsibility for transforming the conflict by speaking openly to one another. The transfer of responsibility and power had begun.

The change was transformational, and delegation after delegation spoke of taking such a process back to their parishes. The beginnings of a new way of being had begun to emerge. The leadership had given direction and retained authority, but had shared decision-making power.

Sharing power

For Bishop Raphael Hess and his diocese in South Africa, forming partnerships and sharing power have been key to how they Live Reconciliation. They see this "Indaba infiltration and infection" spreading through the diocese and raising the level of conversation a few notches. For example, the Finance and Trust Boards have changed the lens through which they look at their work: they are now "men and women focused on mission talking about money."[7] The language and principles of Indaba are also permeating other parts of the diocese, from how the bishop addresses his ordinands on retreat to how the youth meet and make use of their voice across the diocese. The bishop doesn't think that he and the diocese have solved everything, but they have a vision and direction rooted in journeying together.

Distinctive facilitation

Bishop Hess talks of the need to be open to facilitation if we are to take Indaba seriously as a process of Living Reconciliation.

For both power-holders and those who feel they have no power in the situation, trusting the process to a "stranger" can create a sense of vulnerability and risk. But skillful facilitation is essential to create and maintain safe space and to ensure that all voices are heard and relationships honored.

The four Continuing Indaba journeys we have described brought people together from different perspectives and cultures to develop relationships that might bring about honest conversation. They traveled thousands of miles together on intense journeys that were marked by moments of joy and frustration. However, the purpose of these journeys was more than making friends with people different from themselves. After encountering one another's contexts they were brought together for a facilitated conversation. This was not a test to see how they had changed, but an opportunity to explore their diversity within the safety of the relationships they were building. Good facilitation was necessary for this. As one participant explains:

> When we were helped to leave our comfortable, familiar perspectives and enter perspectives and places different to our own something happened that was of God. We developed more of the capacity to fulfil the second part of the greatest commandment...In order to live out the theology of reconciliation and the aspirations of Continuing Indaba, we

had to drill down even further to discover two key elements that made the difference: Willingness and facilitation.[8]

Good facilitation allows an authentic conversation to emerge and for power to be shared. One of the Continuing Indaba facilitators, Kim Barker from South Africa, found the co-facilitation of the final conversation in Jamaica both challenging and rewarding. As she looks back on the process, she writes:

> Facilitating an Indaba conversation is perhaps one of the most challenging facilitation tasks I have undertaken in terms of its intensity and uncertainty, but it was also profoundly rewarding. What am I taking away? Hope. A hope that comes from witnessing people with sincerely held, but opposing beliefs, enter into respectful conversation and remain in conversation, listening long and deeply enough to come to an understanding of the 'other's' position. I am left with a renewed appreciation for the richness that arises from diversity within a faith community, when everyone has a voice, a safe space in which to speak and a company of witnesses who will receive their speaking. We are all impoverished whenever there are voices which struggle to be heard.[9]

Authentic conversation across many differences in culture, viewpoint, and status was made possible only through the skills of facilitators from outside the groups who could identify what was needed for the next step of their journey together and help them get there surely and safely.

Living Reconciliation in your parish

One of the challenges for those who were part of the Continuing Indaba journeys was how to translate what they had learned and the energy they had gained from the experience into their everyday lives. We have described how dioceses can and have been transformed by Living Reconciliation in the way they work and in how people relate to one another. If Living Reconciliation really is at the heart of who we are as Christians, then it is crucial for parish life together. Julian and Cath Hollywell were part of the Diocese of Derby team that journeyed together with the Dioceses of New York and Mumbai. For them the desire to use Living Reconciliation in their own parish where Julian is the vicar, St. Werburgh's in Spondon (England),[10] needed to be rooted and to grow out of their local context. As Cath, now an ordinand, explains:

> A major obstacle to using Indaba lay in thinking that Indaba processes are only used for conflict resolution. Why would we need a process of reconciliation when on the surface

at least there appeared to be little conflict? Spondon has not experienced the violence and division that exist elsewhere in the Anglican Communion. There were no apparent great divides around the ordination of women to the episcopate or issues in human sexuality. There were no apparent great conflicts in the congregation between different families and different parts of the community. But what did exist, as it does in so many churches, is the tendency in all of us to sit in the same place. Literally. To carry on doing the same things in the same way with the same people who we naturally "get along with." The Sunday attendance remained around a steady 120.[11]

Cath's description points out a situation that is a common part of church life in many parishes and congregations not only in England but also in North America and elsewhere. But her experience as part of a Continuing Indaba team brought a new insight:

It was in Bangalore in India after weeks of travelling and getting to know each other as an incredibly diverse group that finally the penny dropped. If our church was going to grow and not just in terms of numbers, then we needed to help each other step out of our relationship comfort zones and cross over barriers which in our case at St. Werburgh's meant crossing over the pews. We discovered that Indaba wasn't only about crossing continents, cultural, and theological divides, but also about crossing over the pews in our own church and that sometimes this would be even more of a challenge. It is after all much easier to shake one another's hand at the sign of peace and just leave it at that. Being reconciled with one another in our congregation meant being willing to really see and hear each other and then being willing to live with our inevitable differences which quite frankly was a very good reason for avoiding reconciliation. I mean who needs that? Who needs that risk in church? Well the surprising answer was, "We do!"

She also describes how this experience was carried home and given root in their own setting at St. Werburgh's:

Between twenty and thirty people regularly sign up and attend groups based on the Indaba process and whilst this isn't the only reason, it is clearly a key reason behind our Sunday attendance growing from 120 to 160 since we began. Apart from contributing to the growth in numbers, these groups have also become a powerful tool in enabling discipleship. It appears that just as it did in New York and Mumbai when we provide "safe" spaces in which our perceptions of people and God are challenged and expanded then the Holy Spirit is allowed to flow and do its work and it happens through others. Time and again in our groups people teach each other just by speaking and just by listening. We regularly prepare for God speaking through the most unlikely person who we might have nothing in common with, and then when it happens (as it often does) the pews disappear. For a moment at least there isn't an "us" or a "them" or even a "me" and a "you" but only God sat there in the circle in the speaker and the listener.

The energy for Living Reconciliation came from a desire to bring peace into a world scarred by violence and ends with a story of church growth in a parish in the Church of England. This is the great story of reconciliation: all global mission takes place in a particular location. All mission is local, but also all mission is global. In transforming our own communities we are participating in the mission of God throughout the world.

Over to you

All the people whose stories are featured in this book are ordinary people who have caught a vision. Whether this is

Peter or Justa, Alice or Rob, they all set out on a journey that has transformed local communities and the world. The hope they have before them is that in Christ the victory has been won, and the dissatisfaction within them is that the world is not as it should be.

If you know this hope and feel this pain, then the opportunity is there for you to partner with others in this journey. There is a relationship between conflicts over relatively small things and the great conflicts of the world. Ultimately they are all between people. They are all transformed by humble actions, sharing hospitality, engaging in genuine conversation, and discovering that those who seemed so strange or difficult are actually our sisters and brothers.

Living Reconciliation is not a program. But within organizations, it is necessary to develop communal responses. When leadership emerges that shares power and trusts people to speak for themselves, the barriers that separate us come tumbling down. When we reorder our churches in this way, we become agents of change in our local setting and in the world. In building relationships with people we once considered as outsiders, we are also able to discover Christ in them, and they are able to discover Christ in us. Social transformation, evangelism, discipleship, and service are not alternatives or extras; they are a holistic mission that can only be effectively entered into together.

Jesus called his disciples to go to the ends of the world. They had no idea where this was. But at the time he spoke, two large islands in the southwest Pacific may have remained undiscovered by any humans. They are called Aotearoa by those who first inhabited them and are known to most of us today as New Zealand. In the 1830s, Church Missionary Society missionaries arrived from England, no doubt carrying with them the ludicrous ideas of European superiority. The Maori—the people of the land—were to be converted not only to Christ but also to a whole cultural understanding of life that included what to wear and how to build new structures, especially how to build churches. The Maori were regarded as children to be instructed, not as people who had the Spirit within them. As with so many missions before and after, the missionaries began by establishing schools. If the children could read in English, the whole Maori culture could be washed away in a generation.[12]

Among the first recruits was a twelve-year-old girl called Tarore from the Ngati Haua tribe. She was bright and able and loved a copy of the Gospel of Luke that she had been given. She had recounted the story of Jesus to her family in Maori, and she kept the book by her side at all times. In 1836 troubles in the area persuaded the missionaries to close the station and evacuate the school to Tauranga. Tarore's father, Ngakuku, and CMS missionary John Flatt led a party of children over the Kaimai Range. The journey took them to the Wairere Falls where they made camp. The campfire attracted a raiding party from Rotorua, led by a man named Uita. Those in the camp responded quickly, and after some fighting the raiding party withdrew. In the confusion, Tarore had been left where she had fallen asleep. When Ngakuku and the others returned to the camp, they found that Tarore had been killed, still on her sleeping mat.

Her death immediately created a desire for *utu*—for revenge. But at her funeral the next day her father preached against revenge, saying there had been too much bloodshed already and that the people should trust in the justice of God.

When Tarore was killed, Uita had taken her copy of the Gospel of Luke, thinking that it might be of value. Since he was unable to read, it remained unopened until a slave, named Ripahau, who could read, was brought to the village. He read to the people from the gospel. Hearing the gospel being read led Uita to send a message asking if he could visit the church at Ngakuku's village to worship and to confess his faith in God. After some hesitation from Ngakuku's people, his request was granted. He arrived at the village a visibly changed man and asked Ngakuku in great humility to forgive him. They knelt in the little church and prayed together.

Tarore's Gospel of Luke did not remain in Uita's village. It went with Ripahau when he left, who used it to teach Tamihana Te Rauparaha and Matene Te Whiwhi to read. In time Tamihana and Matene became Christians; they took Tarore's gospel with them when they traveled to the South Island in December

1842, preaching the gospel of peace and reconciliation among the peoples there.

In 1844 Tamihana accompanied Bishop George Selwyn on his first missionary journey to the South Island of New Zealand. Bishop Selwyn was amazed to find tribes living at peace and following Jesus in discipleship. The missionary became the guest, and discovered that the gospel had gone before him.

The prevailing mood among Victorian missionaries was that the key to their work was individual, personal salvation. They were expecting a conversion not only to Christianity but also to their own cultural expectations of "civilization." At baptism converts were expected to adopt a "Christian" name, but for the missionaries this meant European names. The Maori converts who carried the gospel to the South Island did not take foreign cultural expectations with them. They instead took with them the idea of conversion within the context of their culture, and also of building reconciled communities that would forgo a culture of revenge. This wider vision of the power of the gospel enlightened the hearts of some of the European missionaries.

It is this gospel of transformation—of individuals and communities — that we embrace as we join the journey to Live Reconciliation. You and your companions will be changed on this journey, as the communities you live, work, and worship in are transformed. It is a journey of a lifetime and beyond. It is a journey together deeper into the heart of God. Along this journey we sing with many voices, from many cultures and in many languages. We sing the South Africa freedom song "Siyahamba" in Zulu; "Pescador de Hombres" in Spanish; "Lift Every Voice and Sing" from African American experience; and in multiple harmonies in the words expressing the foundation of Anglican tradition by Charles Wesley and shared widely:

> Finish then thy new creation:
>   pure and spotless let us be;
> let us see thy great salvation
>   perfectly restored in thee;
>
> Changed from glory into glory
>   till in heaven we take our place,
> till we cast our crowns before thee,
>   lost in wonder, love, and praise.[13]

* * *

Prayer

> Loving God, you invite us into your Story of Love. Strengthen our hearts that we might take the risk of sharing power and reimagine our communities as places of transformation. *Amen.*

Questions to think about

1. What might it mean for you and your church to think differently about being church, as Saldanha Bay did?

2. What would it require in your parish and diocese for you collectively to Live Reconciliation?

3. Are you ready to participate in the change? Is your church ready?

Further thinking

For additional material on the topics discussed in this chapter—including videos, study guides, and further reading—please visit www.living-reconciliation.org.

Glossary

Alpha Course: A widely used program that seeks to introduce people to the basics of the Christian faith through an invitation to a meal and discussion. See http://www.alpha.org/.

Anglican Communion: The collective name for autonomous and interdependent churches around the world who affiliate with one another through their common respect for the Archbishop of Canterbury, their participation in the Anglican Consultative Council, and in the Lambeth Conference. There are thirty-eight such churches and each has a primate whom the Archbishop of Canterbury invites to a formal meeting. All churches share common history in their form of worship and are episcopal—led by bishops—who govern with lay and ordained people.

Anglican Consultative Council: The Anglican Consultative Council (ACC) is the most representative body of gathered Anglicans. It is made up of lay people, bishops, priests, deacons, and religious. The meetings are held around the world every three to four years. The ACC has bylaws and a constitution, and through its networks and programs, it seeks to serve the varying needs of member churches on an international scale.

Baraza: A Swahili word for a process similar to Indaba.

church governance structures: The Anglican Communion is made up of autonomous churches, each with their own governance structures. Each church or province is made up of dioceses, which are geographic collections of parishes, missions, or congregations. Each of these is governed by a parochial church council or a vestry. Dioceses and provinces meet at a synod, a convention, or a governing body, which makes decisions on issues in the life of the church.

comfort zone: A physical and psychological space where a person or group feels safe and unchallenged.

conflict transformation: The process by which conflicts may be transformed into peaceful outcomes through structural change such as developing relationships rather than separating disagreeing or warring parties and negotiating mediation.

Continuing Indaba: Initially a project of the Anglican Communion to foster mutual listening, it has developed with official backing into a process to help Anglicans worldwide to live reconciliation by facing our own conflicts, celebrating our diversity and difference, and thereby becoming agents of God's reconciling mission in the world.

convenor: A significant person or body who has the relational authority to call diverse people to participate in a transformative process without determining outcomes.

convention: See church governance structures.

design group: A representative group of people who work with a convenor to design a process that will foster the development of relationships across diversity so that conflict can be transformed.

diocese: See church governance structures.

East African Revival: An important lay-led renewal movement within African Anglicanism in East Africa during the late 1920s and 1930s. It emerged from the dissatisfaction within the colonial church in Uganda and Rwanda. It was inspired by lay members of the Rwanda Mission, who promoted personal holiness as understood by the Keswick movement. African adherents spread the Revival through Rwanda and Uganda to Congo, Tanzania, and Kenya from the 1930s onwards. It is still an important movement in Africa today.

facilitated conversation: Structured conversation where all involved respect the leadership of a facilitator. The aim of the conversation can be to find consensus, negotiate settlement, or to transform conflict.

facilitator: A person who makes possible conversation aimed at fulfilling the desires of the participants, rather than to impose their own solutions.

Faith in Conflict: An ecumenical conference held in Coventry in 2013 on reconciliation. For more, see http://faithinconflict.com.

GAFCON: The Global Anglican Futures Conference (GAFCON) gathered in 2008 as an alternative voice to the Lambeth Conference. This has now become a movement, based on a statement of faith, for conservative Anglicans. See http://gafcon.org.

Indaba: A Zulu word describing a community process for discernment on matters of significance. Such processes are common throughout Africa, Asia, the Pacific islands and the Indigenous peoples of the Americas. Their aim is to further community life, not to solve issues.

indigenous people: A wide term that covers groups of people native to a particular place. There is no cover-all definition for Indigenous people but some characteristics are:

- they tend to have small populations relative to the dominant culture of their country;
- they have (or had) their own language;
- they have distinctive cultural traditions that are still practiced; and
- they have (or had) their own land to which they are tied in many ways.

Lambeth I.10: The resolution passed at the 1998 Lambeth Conference regarding Human Sexuality. See more at: http://www.lambethconference.org/resolutions/1998/1998-1-10.cfm.

Lambeth Commission on Communion: This was set up in 2003 following the consecration of an openly gay and partnered bishop in The Episcopal Church, the authorization of services of blessing of same-sex unions in one diocese of the Anglican Church of Canada, and the absorbing of dissenting parishes in those countries into Anglican Provinces in Africa and South America and thereby challenging the geographic nature of dioceses. Its objective was to consider how the churches of the Anglican Communion could maintain the highest degree of communion among themselves. The Commission published its findings as the Windsor Report (see below).

Lambeth Conference A gathering of the bishops and their spouses from every province of the Anglican Communion. The Archbishop of Canterbury issues the invitation approximately every ten years. The bishops have often debated and voted upon resolutions, but these have no authority in the Communion unless ratified by each province. For this reason the 2008 Lambeth Conference did not feature resolutions.

LGBT: Shorthand for lesbian, gay, bisexual, and transgender people.

mission: All mission is God's mission. The Anglican Communion breaks that down in the five marks of mission:
- to proclaim the good news of the kingdom;
- to teach, baptize and nurture new believers;
- to respond to human need by loving service;
- to seek to transform unjust structures of society, to challenge violence of every kind and to pursue peace and reconciliation; and
- to strive to safeguard the integrity of creation and sustain and renew the life of the earth.

See www.anglicancommunion.org/ministry/mission/fivemarks.cfm.

parochial church council (PCC): See church governance structures.

pilot conversations: The four international Indaba conversations organized by the Anglican Communion Office. The full story of these conversations can be found in the report 'Creating Space' at http://continuingindaba.com/resources/.

primates: In each province of the Anglican Communion one bishop is nominated as primate through election or selection. The role of a primate within his or her own church varies greatly depending on the constitution of that church. Every two or three years, each is invited by the Archbishop of Canterbury to a Primates' Meeting. The primates have no authority as a "body" and their own churches determine how their ministry is carried out in that context.

province: See church governance structures.

safe space: A physical and psychological space where a person or group can express themselves without fear of being made to feel unwelcome, uncomfortable, or unsafe. Creating safe space is usually referred to in the context of minorities and oppressed groups.

synod: See church governance structures.

transcultural: The experience of crossing from one culture to another.

vestry: See church governance structures.

Windsor Continuation Group: Commissioned in 2007 to monitor developments from the Windsor Report, this group reported to the Primates' Meeting in 2009 and recommended the development of mutual listening as a key response to strengthen the Anglican Communion. Their report can be found here at http://aco.org/commission/windsor_continuation/index.cfm.

Windsor Report: The report of the Lambeth Commission on Communion. Published in 2004, it set out theological principles that underlay Communion, defined the mechanisms that hold the Communion together, and made specific recommendations. See http://www.anglicancommunion.org/windsor2004/index.cfm

world-view: Behavior and attitudes are shaped by the way we view the world. Every culture has a different world-view—the shared assumptions upon which decisions are based.

Notes

Foreword

1 Karl Barth, *Church Dogmatics*, IV, 3.2 (Edinburgh: T & T Clark, 1962), p. 607.

Introduction

1 The Episcopal Church (TEC) has dioceses in fourteen different countries although its headquarters is in New York. It will be referred to as The Episcopal Church in this book.

2 *The Report of the Lambeth Conference 1978* (London: CIO Publishing, 1978), pp. 115-24.

3 *The Truth Shall Make You Free—The Lambeth Conference 1988*, (London: Anglican Consultative Council, 1988), pp. 13-17.

4 Robert Eames, *The Eames Commission: The Official Reports* (Toronto: Anglican Book Center, 1994); *The Inter-Anglican Theological and Doctrinal Commission, The Virginia Report*. London: Anglican Consultative Council, 1997. http://www.lambethconference.org/1998/documents/report-1.pdf

5 "From Indaba to Reflections: Timely issues to be addressed in 'purposeful' discussion in Canterbury," July 4, 2008. http://www.lambethconference.org/lc2008/news/news.cfm/2008/7/4/From-Indaba-to-Reflections

6 *The Windsor Continuation Group*, Report to the Archbishop of Canterbury, December 17, 2008. http://www.aco.org/commission/windsor_continuation/docs/WCG%20Report%20Final%20090105.pdf.

1. Living Reconciliation

1 "The Nobel Peace Prize for 2004." http://www.nobelprize.org/nobel_prizes/peace/laureates/2004/press.html.

2 Desmond Tutu, "Nobel Lecture," December 11, 1984. http://www.nobelprize.org/nobel_prizes/peace/laureates/2004/press.html.

3 "From Indaba to Reflections" (see Intro. n. 5)

4 The Rev. John Mark Odour, "Exploring the Baraza Model for Conflict Resolution: The Luo Drumbeat," in *Creating Space*, eds. Canon Phil Groves and Canon Jonathan Draper, Second Edition (London: Anglican Communion Office, 2010), p.89.

5 Bishop John Simalenga, the late Bishop of Central Tanganyika in Tanzania and one of the facilitators during the Continuing Indaba project, speaking at the theological consultation in Limuru, Kenya, October 15-17, 2009.

6 Peter begins as a disciple (literally, one who follows; see Mark 3:13–19) but things change when Jesus appoints him as one of the Twelve Apostles (literally, one who is sent out; see Mark 6:6–13).

7 In Mark 6:45–52 and John 6:16–21 the authors recount the story of Jesus walking on water and the fear of the disciples, but it is in Matthew 14:22–33 alone that Peter's story is told.

8 For Peter's denial of Jesus, see Mark 14:27-31, 66–72. For the post-resurrection account of Jesus appearing to the disciples when they are fishing, see John 21:7–19.

2. Journey into uncertainty

1 *Toward an Understanding of the Purpose and Scope of the Primates' Meeting—A Working Document.* Approved by the Primates Meeting, January 29, 2011, lines 46-47. http://www.aco.org/communion/primates/resources/downloads/prim_scpurpose.pdf

2 John 6:68–69.

3 Luke 10:25-37.

4 Justin Welby, Sermon preached at the Faith in Conflict conference, Coventry, England, February 26-28, 2013, http://www.archbishopofcanterbury.org/articles.php/5023/archbishops-address-at-faith-in-conflict-conference.

5 Max Warren, *Partnership: The study of an idea.* (London: S.C.M. Press, 1956), p. 87.

6 *Celebrating a Journey*, Report on the Continuing Indaba pilot project, available at http://continuingindaba.files.wordpress.com/2012/05/continuing-indaba-report.pdf.

3. Companions

1 Warren, *Partnership*, p. 87.

2 K.C. Hanson, "The Galilean Fishing Economy and the Jesus Tradition," *Biblical Theology Bulletin* 27 (1997), pp. 99–111. This gives a thorough overview of the taxes paid by fishermen and how they were collected. http://www.kchanson.com/ARTICLES/fishing.html.

3 See John 4:7-42 for the entire story.

4 Verse 27. They "were astonished" (the imperfect of *thaumázo* implies more than just a sudden shock or momentary surprise—it is ongoing amazement and wonder).

5 *Celebrating a Journey*, p. 19.

6 "Towards a Strategic Plan: The address of the Rt. Rev. Andrew M.L. Dietsche to the Convention of the Diocese of New York," November 9, 2013. http://www.dioceseny.org/pages/535--2013-bishop-s-address.

4. Encounter with power

1 Voting rights remain an issue in some states. Many names have been used to refer to the peoples who lived on the continent prior to the arrival and settlement of Europeans and others, in addition to the names of their own tribes. Some generic names such as American Indian or Native American are accepted by some but not others. Indigenous currently is more broadly accepted.

2 Paul Tillich, *Love, Power, and Justice* (New York: Oxford University Press, 1954), pp. 84–85, quoted in Max Warren, *Partnership: The study of an idea* (London: SCM Press, 1956), p. 14.

3 This incident was retold by Bishop Festo Kivengere on many occasions and is cited as a moment of clarity for him in R.K. MacMaster and D.R., Jacobs, *A Gentle Wind of God: The influence of the East Africa revival* (Scottdale, PA: Herald Press, 2006), p. 265. This version of the event is as remembered by Phil Groves from a conversation with Bishop Kivengere in May 1985.

4 MacMaster and Jacobs, *A Gentle Wind of God.*

5. Transforming conflict

1 The Rev. John Mark Odour, "The Luo Drumbeat for the Baraza Model." http://continuingindaba.com/2012/06/01/the-luo-drumbeat/

2 Odour,"The Luo Drumbeat."

3 Odour, "The Luo Drumbeat."

4 Odour, "The Luo Drumbeat."

5 William Shakespeare, *Henry V*, Act III, Scene I. http://www.shakespeare-online.com/plays/henryv_3_1.html

6 Odour, "The Luo Drumbeat."

7 Odour, "The Luo Drumbeat."

8 Odour, "The Luo Drumbeat."

9 Odour, "The Luo Drumbeat."

10 Odour, "The Luo Drumbeat."

11 Odour, "The Luo Drumbeat."

12 Richard Gehman, *Learning to Lead: The making of a Christian leaders in Africa* (Nairobi: Oasis International, 2008), p. 67.

13 Odour, *The Luo Drumbeat.*

14 Andrew F. Walls, *The Ephesian Moment: The cross-cultural process in Christian history* (Maryknoll, NY: Orbis Books, 2002), p. 75.

15 Walls, *The Ephesian Moment*, p. 75.

16 Walls, *The Ephesian Moment*, p. 75.

6. Risk

1 Emily Onyango, *Flight: Beginning of the listening process*, http://continuingindaba.com/2012/05/31/flight-beginning-of-the-listening-process/.

2 Onyango, *Flight.*

3 *Celebrating a Journey*, p. 15 (see chap. 2, n. 6)

4 Suzanne Lawson, speaking during the Continuing Indaba presentation to the Anglican Consultative Council, Auckland, New Zealand, November 5, 2011.

5 Lawson, Continuing Indaba presentation.

6 The Indigenous community at St. Philip's uses the name "First Nations."

7 For the full text of Resolution I.10, see http://www.lambethconference.org/resolutions/1998/1998-1-10.cfm

7. New way of being

1 Richard Kerr, "Embracing the Stranger," *Lion and Lamb: Racism and religious liberty*, Autumn 2004. Excerpt cited in "Reflections on what the Bible says: Repentance, humility, inclusion and advocacy," http://www.embraceni.org/christian-response/what-the-bible-says/reflections-on-what-the-bible-says/.

2 Ken Gnanakan and D'zac Niringiye, "The Five Marks of Mission: To Proclaim the Good News of the Kingdom (ii)," in *Mission in the Twenty-First Century: Exploring the five marks of global mission*. eds. Andrew Walls and Cathy Ross (London: Darton, Longman and Todd, 2008), pp. 22-23.

3 Roland Allen, *Missionary Methods: St. Paul's or ours?* (Grand Rapids, MI: Eerdmans, 1962), p. 142.

4 See CI admin, "The Bible and Polygamy in Tanzania," Continuing Indaba, July 28, 2012. http://www.continuingindaba.com/2012/07/18/the-bible-and-polygamy-in-tanzania/.

8. Sharing the vision

1 CI admin, "Indaba—A new way of being: In conversation with Bishop Raphael," October 30, 2013. http://continuingindaba.com/2013/10/30/feature-in-conversation-with-bishop-raphael/

2 Gordon D. Fee, *Paul's Letter to the Philippians*, New International Commentary on the New Testament (Grand Rapids, MI: Eerdmans, 1995), pp. 231–237.

3 Fee, *Paul's Letter to the Philippians*.

4 The Rt. Rev. Andrew M.L. Dietsche, "Installation Sermon," The Cathedral Church of Saint John the Divine, New York, February 2, 2013. <http://www.dioceseny.org/news_items/243-bishop-dietsche-s-installation-sermon>

5 Dietsche, "Installation Sermon."

6 Dietsche, "Installation Sermon."

7 CI admin, "Indaba—A new way of being."

8 Catherine Hollywell, "The World is Only Changed Transforming Their Own Communities," Unpublished paper. March, 2014.

9 *Celebrating a Journey*, p.17.

10 St. Werburgh's, an Anglo-Catholic parish, is part of the United Kingdom's Inclusive Church Network.

11 Hollywell, "The World is Only Changed by Ordinary People."

12 This story was told at the 2012 Anglican Consultative Council meeting held in New Zealand. It also can be found in the *New Zealand Prayer Book*. http://www.anglican.org.nz/content/download/512/4016/file/1910.rtf

13 Charles Wesley, "Love Divine," verse 4, in Hymns for those that Seek, and those that Have Redemption (Bristol, 1747).